CONTAGIOUS FAITH

Discover Your Natural Style for

Sharing Jesus with Others

MARK MITTELBERG

ZONDERVAN REFLECTIVE

Contagious Faith
Copyright © 2021 by Mark Mittelberg

Requests for information should be addressed to:
Zondervan, 3900 Sparks Dr. SE, Grand Rapids, Michigan 49546

Zondervan titles may be purchased in bulk for educational, business, fundraising, or sales promotional use. For information, please email SpecialMarkets@Zondervan.com.

ISBN 978-0-310-11328-7 (softcover)
ISBN 978-0-310-11330-0 (audio)
ISBN 978-0-310-11329-4 (ebook)

Author is represented by the literary agent Don Gates @ The Gates Group, *www.the-gates-group.com.*

Cover Design: Brian Bobel Design
Cover Image: © vchal / istockphoto
Interior Design: Denise Froehlich

Printed in the United States of America

21 22 23 24 25 /LSC/ 10 9 8 7 6 5 4 3 2 1

Mark Mittelberg thinks intentionally about evangelism probably more than anyone else I know. His insights are always biblical and creative. That's why I read everything he writes. I highly recommend this newest book, *Contagious Faith*. It's filled with practical advice on how to share your faith in these days.

RICK WARREN, founding and senior pastor of Saddleback
Church, author of *The Purpose Driven Life*

Contagious Faith is my favorite book on evangelism. It is so empowering to know, as Mark explains, that God has wired us uniquely with different ways of doing evangelism. Whether you are an introvert or extrovert, a thinker or a feeler, this book will give you practical ways of sharing your faith that reflect how God has made you to help build his kingdom.

SEAN MCDOWELL, PhD, speaker, professor at Biola
University, coauthor of *Evidence that Demands a Verdict*

We have the beautiful gift of salvation, but many of us are intimidated about sharing it with others. In *Contagious Faith*, Mark Mittelberg will show you how to use your talents, gifting, and personality for the glory of God. Winsome, accessible, and jam-packed with solid information!

ALISA CHILDERS, host of the Alisa Childers Podcast,
author of *Another Gospel? A Lifelong Christian Seeks
Truth in Response to Progressive Christianity*

Churches have either forgotten that seeking and saving the lost was Christ's mission or they simply don't know how to be effective at it. Mark has laid out the most in-depth strategy for churches and individuals to share the gospel. It has been a game changer at my home church—Christ Church in northeast Louisiana!

WILLIE ROBERTSON, CEO of Duck Commander and
Buck Commander, star of A&E's Duck Dynasty

You are holding more than a book in your hand. You are holding a match that can spark a revival fire that will ignite a family, a community, a workplace, a school, and even a whole nation with the glory and power of God. If you'll read and apply the practical wisdom in *Contagious Faith*, there's no telling how God will work in and through your life.

MATT BROWN, evangelist, founder of Think
Eternity, author of *Truth Plus Love*

Mark is one of my faith heroes and, I believe, among the most important writers of our time. *Contagious Faith* is a masterpiece that combines a biblical rationale with practical counsel and dozens of real-life stories. A powerful guide for discovering the kind of "inner evangelist" I am, I'm confident it will help you discover the same for yourself.

RASHAWN COPELAND, evangelist, founder of Blessed
Media, author of *Start Where You Are*

Mark Mittelberg's wonderful new book, *Contagious Faith*, is a joy to read! Highly motivational and a much-needed reminder that God delights in using all of us who follow Jesus. In a time when people are desperate for good news, *Contagious Faith* helps us share the Best News Ever!

REBECCA MANLEY PIPPERT, author of *Out of the Saltshaker and Into the
World* and *Stay Salt: The World Has Changed, Our Message Must Not*

The greatest evangelistic tool you have at your disposal is you. Effective evangelism happens by employing yourself in the service of the King to naturally and contextually engage others with the good news of Jesus Christ. If you don't know how to do this, my friend Mark Mittelberg wrote *Contagious Faith* to help you find your natural approach.

ED STETZER, executive director, Wheaton College Billy Graham Center

In *Contagious Faith*, Mark doesn't bring us another trend. He brings us a foundation for evangelism you'll want to act upon and then share with your friends. His five Faith Styles will surely get you thinking and, more importantly, acting.

CAREY NIEUWHOF, author of *At Your Best*, podcaster and speaker

We know we should share our faith with others but often struggle with a sense of inadequacy, not knowing where to begin. In this book, Mark Mittelberg gives us the inspiration and practical tools we need to reach others with the gospel. He also reminds us that we are uniquely created by God—gifted to share Jesus in different ways.

DR. MICHAEL L. BROWN, host of the Line of Fire radio broadcast, author of *Answering Jewish Objections to Jesus*, 5 volumes

Nothing enhances my witness more than having a good relationship of trust with the person I'm sharing the gospel. In this context the one I'm burdened for has the opportunity to observe the fruit of God's Spirit in my life in many different settings. In *Contagious Faith*, Mark helps us understand the variety of ways God works in making our faith real to that person.

JOHNNY HUNT, pastor, author, and former president of the Southern Baptist Convention

My favorite books are the ones by authors who I know are living out what they've written. That's why I highly recommend *Contagious Faith* by my friend Mark Mittelberg. It provides practical ways to live a truly contagious faith—one that those who desperately need Jesus will want to catch!

SHANE PRUITT, national Next Gen director of the North American Mission Board of the Southern Baptist Convention, author of *9 Common Lies Christians Believe*

Mark Mittelberg has done it again. While the Good News of Jesus never loses its power to change lives, we need to find fresh ways to talk about it and be renewed in our passion for doing so. *Contagious Faith* reveals five biblical approaches to sharing our faith that fit who God uniquely made us.

> **KEVIN PALAU**, president and CEO of the Luis Palau Association

For too long we've accepted a version of Christian faith that believers think they can keep to themselves. But this looks nothing like Jesus and it's not found in the Bible. In *Contagious Faith*, my friend Mark Mittelberg leads us on a journey of what it looks like to fall in love with the greatest thing on earth—Jesus—to the point you can no longer keep him to yourself.

> **NICK HALL**, evangelist, founder of Pulse, author of the book *Reset*

Contagious Faith tackles head-on the truth that Jesus calls *every* Christian to share the gospel. If that scares you, then this book is for you. Mark outlines how God can use your unique wiring (yes, *yours*) to reach others for the kingdom. He provides practical tips on maximizing your gifts and personality, and helps you learn from other people's strengths too.

> **GREG STIER**, founder/visionary of Dare 2 Share, author of *Unlikely Fighter: The Story of How a Fatherless Street Kid Overcame Violence, Chaos & Confusion to Become a Radical Christ Follower*

Mark Mittelberg has written a terrific guide on how to share your faith in a way that is responsible, faithful, kind, and plays to your own personal gifts. Whether you're a life-of-the-party extrovert or quietly bookish, you can still have a contagious faith. Mark shows you how!

> **MICHAEL BIRD**, PhD University of Queensland, academic dean and lecturer in theology at Ridley College in Melbourne, Australia

I have known and respected Mark for over three decades and commend his ministry, this new book, and his life-changing vision for contagious faith to every Christian who wants to see more people find and follow Jesus. If you want a partner in helping you learn to share your faith in winsome and effective ways, I can think of no better person than Mark Mittelberg.

KEVIN G. HARNEY, founder and visionary leader of Organic Outreach International, author of the *Organic Outreach* trilogy and *Organic Disciples: Seven Ways to Grow Spiritually and Naturally Share Jesus*

When Jesus locked eyes with his disciples to give the Great Commission mandate, he was looking through them at us—his followers throughout time. *Contagious Faith* is a joyous invitation to join Jesus in reaching our neighbors, both local and global. My advice: handle with care. Once you crack it open, you won't be able to contain its infectious message!

DAVID JOANNES, founder/CEO of Within Reach Global, author of *The Mind of a Missionary and Gospel Privilege*

I love how my friend Mark Mittelberg teaches us natural ways to help spiritually wayward sons and daughters find their way back to the Father, and to give them a rock-solid assurance through the gospel that surely heaven waits for them.

KERRY LIVGREN, founding member/songwriter for the band Kansas, writer of "Carry On Wayward Son"

To Effa Mittelberg, whose contagious
faith influenced her entire family for
five generations . . . and counting.

And to O. H. "Mitt" Mittelberg, whose walk
with Christ marked my life . . . for eternity.

*I am grateful for the "sincere faith, which first
lived in [my] grandmother [Effa] and in [my
father, Orland] and, I am persuaded, now
lives in [me, my children, and beyond]."*

—2 TIMOTHY 1:5, PARAPHRASED

CONTENTS

Foreword by Lee Strobel xi

OUR CONTAGIOUS CALLING

1. Reached by God to Reach Others 1
2. Finding an Approach That Fits You 21

THE FIVE CONTAGIOUS FAITH STYLES

3. Style #1: FRIENDSHIP-BUILDING 37
   Key Skills for Every Christian 45

4. Style #2: SELFLESS-SERVING 63
   Key Skills for Every Christian 68

5. Style #3: STORY-SHARING 79
   Key Skills for Every Christian 88

6. Style #4: REASON-GIVING 103
   Key Skills for Every Christian 113

7. Style #5: TRUTH-TELLING 127
   Key Skills for Every Christian 135

8. Understanding and Applying the Gospel. 149

9. When Your Style Doesn't Fit the Situation 169

10. Experiencing the Unexpected Adventure 185

11. Leaving a Lasting Legacy 199

Recommended Resources 211

Notes. 223

Meet Mark Mittelberg .229

FOREWORD

BY LEE STROBEL

Few things deter people from Christianity as much as hypocritical leaders in the church—that is, speakers and authors whose behind-the-scenes lifestyle is antithetical to what they preach from the pulpit or write about in their books.

What's the opposite of a hypocrite? My friend Mark Mittelberg.

Most people only know Mark from his global impact as a sought-after speaker and vigorous champion of personal evangelism. He has trained more people to share their faith than anyone else in his generation. He's considered one of the world's leading authorities on how Christians can naturally talk about Jesus in a way that's winsome and attractive. Churches constantly pursue his insights on how they can become more effective in reaching their community with the gospel.

But I've known the personal side of Mark for more than three decades. As his close friend, I've seen him in countless private moments—in his neighborhood, his home, restaurants, and traveling. And with Mark, what you see in public is what you get in private.

For instance, his friendships in the small Colorado community where he lives has lit the fuse on a mini revival there. As appropriate opportunities have arisen, Mark has faithfully told his neighbors about Jesus, and one by one they have come to faith and been baptized in backyard pools or spas. Then these new believers tell someone else about Jesus, and yet another person is reborn. It's as if faith were—well, *contagious!* Which, of course, is the theme of this book.

In these pages, Mark will help liberate your "inner evangelist." In other words, authentic Christians have a deep desire to see others receive Jesus as their forgiver and leader, but they tend to shrink back from telling them about the gospel because they're uncomfortable with stereotypical approaches to proselytizing.

Mark will reveal how God can use you and your personality to reach out with the gospel in ways that are authentic to who God made you to be. It's an encouraging truth—I don't have to share my faith like you, and you don't have to share it like me. You can be *you*—and God can use *you* to spread his message of hope and grace to one person at a time.

I've seen God use this kind of teaching to transform once-reticent Christians into people who are truly excited about bringing the gospel to friends, neighbors, colleagues, family members, and people they meet along the road of life. Fear dissipates, and Christians become more comfortable in talking about their faith in genuine ways that sync up with their God-given temperament.

Trust me—this book could very well be the launching pad of a newfound life of spiritual adventure for you! In his Sermon on the Mount, Jesus urged us to be salt and light in our increasingly desperate world. He was saying we should live in a way that makes people thirst for God and which shines his message of love and redemption into dark areas of despair.

Discover how you can become *stronger* salt and *brighter* light for the sake of the gospel and the glory of God. Along the way, you'll have the time of your life doing it!

OUR CONTAGIOUS CALLING

"We were meant to live for so much more . . ."

So declares the popular Switchfoot song, *Meant to Live*. The lyrics echo what we are told both by our hearts and God's Word—we really *were* made to live for greater purposes.

More than the typical Christian life. More than just going to school. More than finding a meaningful career. More than the possibility of getting married, having a family, or someday settling down and retiring. And yes, even more than finding God's forgiveness, going to church, and serving others—great as those are.

We were made to know God but also to introduce him to others. To share the love and truth of Jesus with the people around us. To reach them for him. To help them find and follow Christ—and then, in turn, to assist them in helping *others* find and follow Christ as well.

"As the Father has sent me," Jesus declared, "I am sending

you" (John 20:21). And he added, "You will be my witnesses in Jerusalem, and in all Judea and Samaria, and to the ends of the earth" (Acts 1:8).

Our faith is not just for ourselves. It's not to be hoarded. It's meant to be spread to others. To be infectious. *Contagious.*

Why Contagious?

It's a word we've been hearing a lot lately. The world has been swept up in a pandemic, and we've been bombarded with warnings designed to prevent us from catching this highly communicable virus.

Stay home, stay safe. Wear a mask. Stop the spread. In such an environment, there's no more troublesome thought than the fear that you might be contagious.

But amid the cautions to cover coughs and squelch sneezes, I'm reminded of times in my life when I caught something that I couldn't resist—and didn't really want to. Times, for example, when I felt down and defeated, but then a friend's contagious optimism inspired me. There's contagious enthusiasm. Contagious excitement. Contagious laughter.

Contagious isn't always a bad thing. It describes something irresistible, something you can't help but catch, and something you have the potential to spread.

What if our *faith* were contagious? What if instead of quietly clinging to our relationship with Christ and succumbing to the societal sentiment that faith should be private, we realized that faith is for sharing? That Jesus came not just for me and you but to be the Savior of the world—and that he wants us to share the Good News about him with others?

When Jesus gave the Great Commission in Matthew 28:18–20—when he told us to go into all the world to make disciples—he was giving us a mission to share a *contagious faith.* He wanted us to intentionally go into our circles of influence and beyond, telling anyone who would listen about his love and truth. And our goal (borrowing Merriam-Webster's definition of *contagious*) is to *excite similar emotions and conduct in others*[1]— and, I would add, *beliefs* as well.

In so doing, God will use us to infectiously spread our faith to a few other people who will, in turn, carry it to others, who will then relay it to still more. In this way, what Jesus unleashed through his handful of disciples on a hillside two millennia ago will be transmitted through us, and through those we reach, until it ultimately expands to the ends of the earth. In fact, Jesus promised that before he returns, "this gospel of the kingdom will be preached in the whole world as a testimony to all nations" (Matthew 24:14).

It's a lofty vision, but also an exceedingly important and fulfilling one. And it's for all of us who name Christ as our forgiver and leader. More than that, it's a thrilling journey—the most exciting and rewarding thing we can do with our lives.

That said, I understand—you're not so sure about your role in all of this . . . *yet!*

At one time I wasn't sure about my role in it either. But read on, friend. You're in for a wonderful journey. Dare I say, *an unexpected adventure.*

CHAPTER 1

REACHED BY GOD TO
REACH OTHERS

Be wise in the way you act toward outsiders;
make the most of every opportunity.

—COLOSSIANS 4:5

Why me? I wondered.

Why would God ask someone like me—who just weeks ear-lier had been recklessly partying and resisting him—to be the one to talk about spiritual stuff to someone like Peggy?

It wasn't that I didn't want to encourage her. We had been friends in high school, we were on the drama team and in a few of the same plays, and we'd even been at some parties together. But now my life had changed radically. I'd trusted in Christ, though I wasn't quite sure what that was going to look like.

Peggy had recently started visiting a Bible study that I attended, and I'd been sensing that God wanted me to talk to her about it. I couldn't get away from the concern that she was becoming acclimated to our Christian culture but missing the central point of what it means to become a true follower of Christ.

But, again, why me? I barely knew what I was doing. I was only nineteen years old and had put my trust in him less than two months earlier. I had not been trained to share my faith. I hadn't been through any evangelism courses. I felt like a novice when it came to discussing God's activity in my life . . . because, well, I *was* a novice. I just knew that I needed to do so, and I was willing to try—even if it meant feeling awkward in the process.

An Unexpected Adventure

As I was crossing the Eighth Street Bridge in our hometown, I saw Peggy walking alone on the snow-packed sidewalk. I was surprised that anyone would be out for a stroll on such a frigid December day, but I believed this could be the opportunity God had been pointing me toward.

I pulled my car to the side of the road and rolled down the passenger window to say hello (yes, we actually had to *roll down* our windows in those days). We chatted for a few minutes, and then I mentioned the study group. She told me she was enjoying it, loved meeting so many new friends, and was learning from the discussions.

"I'm glad you're growing in your understanding of God and the Bible," I said, as I took a deep breath and tried to sound more confident than I actually felt. "But there's something I've been meaning to ask you."

"What's that?" Peggy replied.

"I'm curious to know . . ." I said, trying to muster the courage to get to the heart of the matter, ". . . whether you've ever really asked for Jesus's forgiveness and committed your life to him?"

"No, I've never done that," Peggy said. "And nobody has ever told me I needed to!"

Trading Places

Let's hit the pause button and trade places. You're talking to your friend and suddenly the conversation shifts from breezy banter to a serious spiritual exchange. She has just told you she's never really understood the offer of the gospel and has never asked to receive salvation through Christ.

What would you say to your friend? Would you "be prepared to give an answer" (1 Peter 3:15) and to explain the core message of the Christian faith? Or would you change the subject and talk about something less intimidating? Would you say something about how important the topic is and suggest raising it at a future Bible study? Would you declare a timeout and call in a professional—maybe a pastor, or at least a more seasoned follower of Christ? Or might you be tempted to suddenly pretend there was an urgent matter elsewhere that you needed to attend to?

Stumbling Forward

Any of those options might have been attractive to me at that point—except for the nagging awareness I had that God had seemingly brought us to this moment and wanted to work through our conversation despite my insecurities.

I'm not sure what I was so afraid of. Maybe I was worried that Peggy would think I was judging her, or that I was trying to push her into a commitment she wasn't ready to make. Or perhaps it was the very real possibility that she would be open and ready to trust in Christ—but I wouldn't say things clearly and instead would squander the opportunity. Whatever the source of my trepidation, it turned out to be an unwarranted concern.

"Well," I replied, feeling a tinge of Holy Spirit-inspired confidence, "you really *do* need to ask Jesus for his forgiveness and leadership in your life." Then I started doing my best to explain what that means, including telling her how I had given my life to Christ just weeks earlier.

To my relief, she seemed receptive—but she also let me know she needed to get back home soon for a family dinner. She quickly added that she'd like to continue talking later that evening, if I'd be willing to swing by. I said I would, and I silently prayed that God would move in her heart, opening her to the gospel.

God Worked—In Spite of Me

When we picked up the discussion later that night, I found out that God had been working in Peggy's life in a variety of ways. She had a formal church background but had walked away from it in junior high. Now, after graduating from high school and spending a summer working at Yellowstone National Park, Peggy had a renewed interest in spiritual matters. In fact, God was speaking to her through a Bible she had "stolen" from a hotel room in Yellowstone (not realizing that the Gideons put them there *hoping* people will "steal" them); through several of her Christian friends; through our Bible study; through a service at a church the night before; and now through our interactions.

By the time our conversation was over, Peggy was ready to

ask Jesus for his forgiveness and guidance in her life. With my heart beating fast, I did my fledgling best to lead her in a coherent prayer of repentance and faith. In spite of my inadequacies, the Holy Spirit worked in a powerful way—and Peggy's life and eternity were changed. What a thrill it was for me to help seal her relationship with God!

And how exhilarating it will be for *you* to be used in similar ways—whether you feel up to the task yet or not!

God Will Work through You

Deep down we all want our lives to count for things that last. But think about this: the only things in this world that we can take with us into eternity are *people*.

Wouldn't you like to be used by God to impact people's lives and eternities? It can happen. But what will it take? What are some of the key truths we'll need to embrace in order to move forward in the adventure of reaching others with the best news the world has ever known?

Let's look at some evangelism essentials. I urge you to approach these prayerfully, asking God's Spirit to guide you concerning any areas you might need to reflect on, pray over, or shore up in your life. These are foundational for your journey toward having a more contagious faith.

Essentials for a Contagious Faith

This Is God's Mission

It's vital for us to understand and embrace this first component. Reaching people with the gospel was not *our* idea. It's not something we came up with and are now asking God to help us accomplish. No, it's the opposite. It was the heavenly Father who "so loved the world that he gave his one and only Son, that whoever believes in him shall not perish but have eternal life" (John 3:16).

It was that Son, Jesus, who willingly "came to seek and to save the lost" (Luke 19:10), and then told us to go into our world to do the same (Matthew 28:18–20). Jesus also promised us the Holy Spirit, from whom we would "receive power," so that we could become his "witnesses in Jerusalem, and in all Judea and Samaria, and to the ends of the earth" (Acts 1:8).

So, *God's* mission of rescuing wayward sons and daughters has now become *our* mission—and fortunately he promises to be with us always, even "to the very end of the age" (Matthew 28:20).

Pastor and author Henry Blackaby reminds his listeners that we need to "watch to see where God is working and join Him in His work." Well, God's work is clearly to reach and redeem people who are far from him. We can have supreme confidence that we are joining him in doing just that, knowing that his gospel is still "the power of God that brings salvation to everyone who believes" (Romans 1:16).

The God of the universe is already on a mission to seek and save the lost—and we have the privilege of joining him in his mission.

This Mission Is for Every Believer

It's tempting to think that God's challenge to reach a lost world is a task that's reserved for elite Christians—those with special gifts or training. But that isn't the case. *We are all members of the church to which Jesus gave the Great Commission.* Specifically, when he locked eyes with his disciples in Matthew 28:19–20, he was looking through them at us—all of his followers throughout time.

"Go and make disciples of all nations," he told us, "baptizing them in the name of the Father and of the Son and of the Holy Spirit, and teaching them to obey everything I have commanded you." And, as we saw earlier, in Acts 1:8 he added, "you will be my witnesses in Jerusalem, and in all Judea and Samaria, and to the ends of the earth."

Yes, these words are for you and me—and for everyone who is a genuine follower of Jesus. They are God's exciting invitation into a divine partnership to change our world. We can't do this without God, but for reasons he doesn't explain, he chooses to do this with and through us.

You'll often feel like you're out of your league. We all do. There are times when you'll be nervous and tempted to keep your mouth shut. I get it. Your heart will be beating fast and your palms will sweat. Join the club. But God knows how to help us, to use us, and to change people's eternities through the divinely directed efforts we'll make.

We Must Have It before We Can Give It Away

There are plenty of nominal ("in name only") Christians who attend our churches and even our classes and small groups. Researcher George Barna and his team, who have studied this phenomenon for decades, have found that, on average, about half of the people who sit in churches each week have never truly trusted Christ. This is a sobering reality—even a frightening one.

More than that, it's a great reason for self-examination. Paul admonished us as members of the church to "examine yourselves to see whether you are in the faith; test yourselves" (2 Corinthians 13:5). Our salvation depends on knowing and trusting the Savior. But it's also critical to the contagion of our faith. After all, you can't give away what you don't genuinely have. As my friend Steve Macchia explains in his book, *Becoming a Healthy Church*, evangelism is best described as *overflow*—it's letting the good we have in Christ spill over into the lives of the people around us.[1] But that means we need to really have it first.

Peter tells us in 1 Peter 3:15 that in our hearts we must "revere Christ as Lord"—meaning we need to make sure he has his proper place as the master of our lives—and *then* we can effectively "be prepared to give an answer to everyone who asks you to give the reason for the hope that you have." Being right with our Savior is the prerequisite; out of that proper relationship he can equip and use us to answer people's questions and impact their lives.

How about you? Are there things you need to address in your relationship with God? "Seek first his kingdom and his righteousness," Jesus told us in Matthew 6:33—and then everything else can flow out of that healthy relationship with him.

Let me urge you: don't gloss over this point. Like David writes in Psalm 139:23–24, come before God and sincerely ask him,

> Search me, God, and know my heart;
>> test me and know my anxious thoughts.
> See if there is any offensive way in me,
>> and lead me in the way everlasting.

Then confess, give up, or change anything he shows you. As honestly and completely as you know how, receive his forgiveness and "sanctify Christ as Lord"—and then let him lead you forward on this great outreach adventure together.

God Can Use Us at Any Stage of Development

Our spiritual enemy, Satan, loves to whisper in our ear that we're not good enough, we don't know enough, or we haven't walked with God long enough for him to really use us.

"Wait until you've gotten all the sin out of your life," he murmurs, while giving you a poignant reminder of the last time you disobeyed God. "And while you're cleaning up your act, you should probably wait until you've read all those religious books you've been stacking up—or better yet, go earn a seminary degree or two. Then God might *finally* be able to do something worthwhile with you."

No wonder Revelation 12:10 calls him "the accuser."

Even the apostle Paul sometimes struggled with weakness and inadequacy. He took these feelings to God who told him, "My grace is sufficient for you, for my power is made perfect in weakness." Paul's conclusion? "Therefore I will boast all the more gladly about my weaknesses, so that Christ's power may rest on me. That is why, for Christ's sake, I delight in weaknesses, in insults, in hardships, in persecutions, in difficulties. *For when I am weak, then I am strong*" (2 Corinthians 12:9–10, emphasis mine).

Paul also warned Timothy to "Be prepared in season and out of season . . . do the work of an evangelist," (2 Timothy 4:2, 5). Here's the truth: most of us feel "out of season" most of the time. But if we'll make ourselves available to him, he knows how to make up the difference, using us at whatever our current stage of development might be.

We Must Be Fueled by Love

God, by his very nature, is love (1 John 4:8). And we, as his children, are to reflect his love. In fact, Matthew tells us that when Jesus saw the crowds, "*he had compassion on them*, because they were harassed and helpless, like sheep without a shepherd" (Matthew 9:36, emphasis mine). Ed Stetzer explains, "the term 'compassion' means the visceral organs—a deep, gut-wrenching affection."[2]

Stetzer also points out that it was Jesus's heartfelt compassion that compelled him to declare in the next two verses, "The harvest is plentiful but the workers are few. Ask the Lord of the harvest, therefore, to send out workers into his harvest field" (verses 37–38). Jesus's loving concern for people led to his desire to commission more and more contagious carriers of his message who would work to reach them.

In addition, Paul says, "Christ's love compels us," and he adds that he "has committed to us the message of reconciliation. We are therefore Christ's ambassadors, as though God were making his appeal through us" (2 Corinthians 5:14, 19–20). See how experiencing the love *of* Christ flows naturally into the work of reaching people *for* Christ? The two go hand in hand.

If you're driven to share your faith by any motivation other than love, then you're running on the wrong fuel. Our mission is ultimately not to win arguments, to prove people wrong, to get them to do what we want them to do, or to join our church or cause. No, it's to lovingly point them to the Savior so that they, too, can experience the love and forgiveness of our gracious God.

Are you sensing God's love in your life these days? Does it encourage you to share his love with others? If not, then let me urge you to make this a matter of prayer, asking him to expand your heart for him and for the people in your life. We can be confident he delights in answering prayers like that.

We Must Be Grounded in God's Truth

It might seem self-evident that we need to be rooted in the teachings of the Bible, but unfortunately that's no longer obvious to some people. More and more self-proclaimed Christians are talking about God and telling people what they think he wants for their lives, but they do so without stopping to consult his actual revelation to make sure they're telling people the right things about him.

For example, many are mistaken about biblical doctrines related to the deity of Christ, the person of the Holy Spirit, and salvation through Christ alone[3]—let alone the moral confusion that spreads through Christian circles about matters of sexuality and marriage. It seems that we are living in that time Paul warned us about, when people would no longer "put up with sound doctrine. Instead, to suit their own desires, they will gather around them a great number of teachers to say what their itching ears want to hear" (2 Timothy 4:3).

"But you," Paul continues, "keep your head in all situations, endure hardship, do the work of an evangelist . . ." (verse 5). In other words, don't succumb to their wishes, but keep holding to, living, and proclaiming the unadulterated teachings of Scripture.

May we never become the kind of people to whom Jesus must say, "Your mistake is that you don't know the Scriptures, and you don't know the power of God" (Mark 12:24 NLT). If you want to serve the true God and make genuine disciples, then you must "do your best to present yourself to God as one approved, a worker who does not need to be ashamed and who correctly handles the word of truth" (2 Timothy 2:15).

"Can the blind lead the blind?" Jesus asked his listeners. "Will they not both fall into a pit? The student is not above the teacher, but everyone who is fully trained will be like their teacher" (Luke 6:40).

If you want to lead others into the faith, then you must first make certain that the faith you're leading them into is anchored in the clear and consistent doctrines of God's Holy Word, the Bible.

We Must Communicate through Both Works and Words

Many believers think that if they just live an authentic Christian life, others will see it and be inexorably drawn to it. But that is, at best, a half-truth. It's correct that our actions really matter, and they can be highly attractive to the people we hope to reach.

Jesus said in Matthew 5:16, for example, that we should let our "light shine before others, that they may see your good deeds and glorify your Father in heaven." But he also told us, as we saw earlier, that we need to go into the world and make disciples, "*teaching them* . . ." (Matthew 28:20, emphasis mine)—which inevitably involves *words*. He modeled this balance as he lived out his earthly ministry, serving people with his works but also teaching them with his words.

Add to this Paul's challenge: "But how can they call on him to save them unless they believe in him? And how can they believe in him if they have never heard about him? And how can they hear about him unless someone tells them?" (Romans 10:14

NLT). I like to paraphrase Paul's point like this: "Your friends are never going to *see it*, unless you go to them and *say it*."

Good works can open hearts; grace-filled words can open minds. The Holy Spirit can use the two elements together to redeem lives for eternity.

Reaching People Is a Process

Those we hope to reach rarely move from spiritual doubt or disinterest all the way over to trust in Christ in one fell swoop. Instead, the journey usually happens over time. My former atheist friend, for example, took almost two years to carefully investigate the evidence for Christianity before becoming a follower of Jesus. One of my former Muslim friends took more than seven or eight years before he made the same decision. There are people in my life who I've been trying to reach for far longer but who don't seem to be spiritually open even now. Therefore, we need to be willing to walk with friends over the long haul as they consider Christ.

Remember that Jesus himself taught that those who were considering following him should first count the cost of becoming his disciple (Luke 14:25–35). In effect, he was urging them to slow down and make sure they knew what they were committing to before signing on with him—and that takes some time.

"But didn't Paul come to faith in Jesus almost instantaneously on the road to Damascus?" some will ask. "If so, why do you say it needs to be a process?"

Yes, he did—and I love it when God intervenes and fast-tracks someone's journey to faith. But that's not the norm. In fact, the example of Paul highlights why, for most people, coming to Christ is a longer process.

Many of the folks we're trying to reach today are much more

secular than the average seeker was in biblical times. Most people back then, like Paul, had a strong belief in the supernatural, so you didn't need to try to convince them that God was real, that there was an afterlife, or that they would be held accountable someday for how they lived. But today we often need to show people why these beliefs make sense—and this requires more time, energy, information, and patience.

Because of such differences in our culture today, I'd recommend that you anticipate this being a longer, step-by-step process. Then do all you can to try to facilitate that process by helping your friends stay on the path as they move toward Christ, until the exciting day when they finally put their trust in him.

Reaching People Is a Team Activity

It's intimidating to think that the process of someone coming to faith in Jesus is all dependent on you. Fortunately, that's almost *never* the case.

God had worked in Peggy's life in a variety of ways—through her summer in Yellowstone, a hotel Bible, several of her out-of-town friends, members of the Bible study group I was a part of, a church service the evening prior—all before I had the privilege of being used by him that night. That's how the Holy Spirit usually works: he wields a variety of resources to help people move toward Christ.

It was the same in Bible times. Paul illustrated this in 1 Corinthians 3:5–6: "What, after all, is Apollos? And what is Paul? Only servants, through whom you came to believe—as the Lord has assigned to each his task. I planted the seed, Apollos watered it, but God has been making it grow." See how the process works? We are simply instruments in God's skillful hands, contributing our own small voice to the symphony he's orchestrating.

My friend Cliffe Knechtle puts this divine partnership in perspective in this way:

> A person's coming to Christ is like a chain with many links . . . There are many influences and conversations that precede a person's decision to convert to Christ. I know the joy of being the first link at times, a middle link usually, and occasionally the last link. God has not called me to only be the last link.[4]

It's encouraging to know that we can each play a unique role (or several roles) in the divine effort God is directing to bring people into his family. This relieves us of the unhealthy burden of thinking that someone else's relationship with God is all on our shoulders.

We just need to be prepared and available, and then "make the most of every opportunity" (Colossians 4:5) as God shows us open doors to spiritually encourage and speak to people for him. As each of us is faithful in doing our part, he will use us together as a team to communicate his purposes of grace and redemption.

Reaching People Is a Spiritual Activity

This final evangelism essential, which reminds us of the *spiritual* side of these efforts, brings us back to the first one. Because this is *God's* mission, we must recognize our need for God's help and lean on his guidance, wisdom, and power as we seek to reach our families and friends for him.

This doesn't diminish the importance of the assignments God gives us in this divine partnership, but it does spotlight the part that's easiest for us to forget. Namely, as Paul explains in Ephesians 6:12, "Our struggle is not against flesh and blood, but against the rulers, against the authorities, against the powers of this dark world and against the spiritual forces of evil in the heavenly realms."

You see, helping people come to Christ is not just a matter of giving them good information or answers to their questions and objections. Neither is it just about being passionate or persuasive—though all of these can be important. It is, at bottom, a spiritual struggle that is being fought at an unseen level, and because of this we are *all* out of our league and need God's wisdom, help, and intervention.

Ultimately it is the Holy Spirit who draws people into God's loving arms. Therefore, we need to be as attuned to him and his workings as we possibly can be. This will come only through spending deep and consistent times with him in prayer, as well as regularly studying God's Word, the Bible.

"If you remain in me and I in you," Jesus promised in John 15:5, "you will bear much fruit." And don't miss his next phrase: ". . . apart from me you can do nothing."

This shouldn't surprise or discourage us; instead, it should drive us to our knees. It should cause us to humbly seek his help, his guidance, his power, and his blessing—for when we're really and truly abiding in him and he in us, then we will "bear much fruit." Pray frequently and fervently for the people in your life who need to know Christ. In so doing, you will activate divine forces and unseen activities that we can barely understand—but which will nevertheless impact eternity.

If praying for all the unbelievers in your life seems overwhelming, start by praying for just one friend who needs to know him (and if you don't know any unbelievers, then *that's* something to pray about). Begin asking God daily to work in that person's heart, opening their eyes to their need for him, drawing them to the salvation he offers, and providing opportunities for you to share your faith with them. Invite them to events, classes, group meetings, or church services where they'll hear more about the love and truth of Jesus and be given the opportunity to put their trust in him.

We Were Made to Live for So Much More

I hope this discussion has increased your excitement for spiritual impact. A life spent following Christ is a good thing, but one spent contagiously spreading the grace of Christ to others is an *extraordinary* thing.

There is nothing more rewarding than knowing that the God of the universe is loving through you, that he is speaking through you, that he is reaching through you, and that he is in the process of changing the lives of precious men, women, and children through your efforts to bring them to him.

We have a breathtaking opportunity in front of us—to share the life- and eternity-altering message of the gospel which, according to Romans 1:16, "is the power of God that brings salvation to everyone who believes." Let's not take this lightly. Let's gear up and get prepared, because he is ready to use us in amazing ways.

What ways? you ask. Let me finish the story I started with.

Ripple Effects of a Contagious Faith

After having the incredible privilege of praying with Peggy to receive Christ on that wintry day so long ago, I was excited to see how she began to grow in her faith, and then share it with others.

But not long after that she relocated to another part of the country, as did I—and we lost touch with each other. I hoped and prayed that she was staying steadfast in her walk with Christ, but I didn't really know.

I didn't get an update until several years later when I was back home for a high school class reunion and talked to one of our mutual friends. I was thrilled to find out that Peggy had married a Christian guy named Wayne—and together they had decided to join Wycliffe Bible Translators and move with their three young children to serve as full-time missionaries in a distant land.

Ironically, my friend who had once pilfered a Bible from a hotel room was now dedicating her life to taking the Scriptures to people on the other side of the globe who needed to hear them in their own language. Peggy and Wayne ended up serving in Papua New Guinea—the world's most linguistically diverse country, with more than 700 native dialects—for twenty-three years. They supported Bible translation work there, ministering to fellow missionaries and investing in the lives of missionary kids as well as Papua New Guineans. Then they returned to the United States to continue serving Wycliffe ministries from here, encouraging others to take God's Word to people all over the world.

But think about this. The God of the universe—who cares about people more than we'll ever be able to—used my nervous, stumbling early evangelistic efforts as part of a series of influences that led a young woman to Christ. Then she married a like-minded man and together they spent almost a quarter of a century sharing the gospel in one of the most remote places in the world, leading people to faith in Jesus and supporting the work of Bible translation so that other language groups could know him as well. Their work continues to ripple through that nation and throughout the world.

And I got to be a small part of that!

And you know what? I'm guessing that someday in heaven, about 37,242 years from now, a sincere young Papua New Guinean might walk up to me (or maybe teleport over to me?), and say, "I just found out something about you, and I wanted to say thank you."

"That's nice," I'll say. "But for what?"

"I just discovered that you helped lead Wayne's wife Peggy to faith in Jesus. Well, Peggy was one of my teachers at Ukarumpa, and she had a big impact on me. Through my relationship with her and other caring missionaries, my entire family and I put our trust in Jesus. She was also a link in the chain of events that led me to become part of Bible translation efforts myself, and as a result even more of my people now know Jesus as Lord and Savior. So, I wanted to express my gratitude for the way you allowed the Holy Spirit to use you to help reach her."

Can you *imagine*?

Seriously, what could be more rewarding? What could be better? What could be more important? What could be more urgent? What else can we invest in that will last forever? In what other ways could small risks turn into changed lives, transformed families, and more and more people headed for eternity with God?

And that's just a foretaste of how God wants to use *you*.

"This is to my Father's glory," Jesus assured us in John 15:8, "that you bear much fruit . . ."

CHAPTER 2

FINDING AN APPROACH THAT FITS YOU

*There are different kinds of gifts, but the same
Spirit distributes them. There are different kinds
of service, but the same Lord. There are different
kinds of working, but in all of them and in
everyone it is the same God at work.*

—1 CORINTHIANS 12:4-6

My wife Heidi and I had just arrived in England for an overseas
summer ministry experience. We had lofty visions of what it
would be like to bring the Good News to people in other parts of
the world. But what we would actually be doing day by day was
still a bit of a mystery. I asked one of the leaders how we would
be spending our time.

"I'm glad you asked!" he said with exuberance. "We're going
to go all around the neighborhoods near the church, knock on
doors, and tell people about Jesus!"

"All day?" I asked, trying to hide my hesitancy.

"*All summer!* It's gonna be great."

Gulp.

Heidi and I had signed up for a summer tour of duty with a wonderful church in the heart of South London. It was filled with believers who had huge hearts for God and were highly motivated to reach out with his love to their neighbors. I was excited by the opportunity to introduce people to Jesus, but the prospect of knocking on strangers' doors day after day was—well, daunting.

I did my best to reassure myself that this was going to be a good experience. *I love God and I love people,* I thought, *and tomorrow I get to go out and meet lots of nice British folks and introduce them to Jesus. This isn't going to be so bad . . .*

By the next morning, my self-directed sermon was having at least some effect. I felt a slight twinge of excitement. But I was about to discover how hard this could be.

You might already suspect what we soon discovered: most British people weren't huge fans of Americans, fresh out of Heathrow Airport, wandering through their neighborhoods and knocking on their doors to tell them about Jesus. Forget having tea and crumpets. We could barely get our foot in the door of most of the houses we called on.

"What do you want?" people would blurt out through their cautiously cracked-open doorways. We would explain we were visiting from the church around the corner and wondered if they'd be interested in talking about spiritual matters. "Oh, well, we're part of a different parish—and we don't have any questions," they would say, closing the door quickly.

One lady even said to me in a mildly accusatory tone, "You have an *American* accent!"

Trying to stay upbeat, I replied, "Well, what a coincidence—we *are* Americans!"

"Then why don't you go home," she replied, "and pester people in your own country?"

Honestly, at the moment that sounded like a pretty good idea!

Tough Times at Trafalgar Square

Then things got even harder. After weeks of knocking on doors, our team captain announced that we'd be joining up with several other London churches and heading downtown to do some "open-air evangelism" in the central part of the city.

Again, I tried to keep a positive attitude. At least we'd be hitting some fresh territory.

The intent was good, but the strategy wasn't adequately thought through. An advance team had set up a small sound system to amplify a local worship leader in hope that his music would attract and intrigue people. But in the land that spawned the Beatles, the Rolling Stones, and Led Zeppelin, the musician's guitar strumming didn't stir up a lot of interest. More challenging yet, our outreach took place on the afternoon of the annual gay march—and their parade route just happened to go around our location in Trafalgar Square. The raucous atmosphere made discussing serious spiritual matters all the more difficult.

We did the best we could, but when we were finally done, I was really DONE. Done with cold calling. Done with knocking on doors. Done with approaching strangers.

Done with evangelism.

After eight weeks of such uphill efforts, my disenchantment followed me home. It wasn't that I was suddenly against evangelism—I was just convinced it wasn't for me. I resolved that in the future I'd serve God in other ways and leave outreach for the outreach types.

A New Discovery

A few weeks later, though, I heard a sermon that made me rethink my resolution.

The pastor challenged the idea that in order to share our faith we have to try to become something we're not, or to imitate the approach someone else is comfortable taking. He explained that God intentionally builds diversity into his church, and he delights to use people with different backgrounds, different cultures, different ethnicities, different spiritual gifts, and different approaches to sharing their faith—all in concert with each other and all to expand his body of believers here on earth.

As he continued the sermon, the pastor gave a number of examples from the New Testament to illustrate that even in the early church they didn't all do evangelism in the same way. He pointed to biblical figures such as Peter and Paul. They were both influential church leaders gifted in sharing the gospel, but they used vastly different approaches to do so.

Peter deployed his hard-hitting personality to present the gospel in direct ways. At times he was even confrontational. For instance, on the Day of Pentecost, Peter challenged his listeners with the truth about Jesus's crucifixion and resurrection, and then he confronted them with their need to "Repent and be baptized . . . in the name of Jesus Christ for the forgiveness of your sins" (Acts 2:38). God powerfully used Peter's bold and unvarnished words as 3,000 people turned to Christ that day.

Then there was the apostle Paul, who used a more intellectual style to present the gospel. We see an example of his approach in Acts 17, where Paul stood up and spoke in the Areopagus in Athens, Greece, to address the Epicurean and Stoic philosophers who, according to the passage, "spent their time doing nothing but talking about and listening to the latest ideas" (verse 21). It was a tough audience, but God used Paul's reasoned approach to get through to some of those scholars who soon "became followers of Paul and believed" (verse 34).

These and several other early Christians were presented as examples who used approaches that were natural to them, and who applied those approaches according to the needs of the moment.

Finding Roles That Fit Us

This sermon had me rethinking those months of trying to reach out to strangers in London. Heidi and I had initially struggled to even get people to talk with us, let alone to discuss spiritual matters. But we noticed that, as we went from door to door (to door), people were more open to Heidi, at least initially, than they were to me. This wouldn't surprise you if you knew her. She's an outgoing "people person" who enjoys making new acquaintances and quickly engaging them in casual conversations.

Recognizing this, we soon decided that *she* would be the one who knocked on the doors. I'd hover behind my five-foot-tall wife until the door would fling wide, and then I'd rush in behind her.

The innovation paid off. Heidi had a natural ability to put people at ease and break the ice in initiating interactions that could then lead to fruitful spiritual discussions. We found ourselves getting invited into homes more regularly, being served tea more frequently, and having meaningful conversations more consistently.

Heidi got us in the door, but when people would ask us a challenging theological question, then it would naturally become my turn. I disliked approaching strangers to try to engage them in serious discourse, but I loved addressing their spiritual questions and objections whenever these weightier matters came up.

That sermon, along with my reflections back on the lessons we'd learned through trial and error during our summer of ministry in London, helped me realize that my interest in giving evidence for Christianity was all about *evangelism*. I was motivated to clear the intellectual pathway for people in order to help them consider Christ and his offer of salvation.

For me, this realization was a revolution. I didn't need to write off evangelism in my own life—far from it! Rather, I needed to find ways to express it more naturally. I discovered that God knew what he was doing when he made me. He gave me my personality on purpose. He didn't create me to be someone who enjoyed walking up to strangers or knocking on doors to tell people about Jesus. Instead, God designed me to be someone who, like Paul, loves to interact with people about their beliefs, to address their questions and objections, and to help remove their intellectual roadblocks—all in order to open them up to the life-changing message of the gospel.

Discovering Your Natural Approach

I believe this information can become revolutionary for you as well.

Maybe you've never tried sharing your faith in ways that don't fit you, like I did that summer in London. But you can at least imagine what it would feel like. Intuitively, none of us wants to be put on the spot or to face situations where we feel out of place or ill-equipped. And from my interactions with many Christians over the years, these kinds of images are what often come to their minds—real or imagined—when they think about getting involved in personal evangelism.

A related barrier we have to sharing our faith is the sense that we'll have to force ourselves to become something we're not, whether positive or negative. Our examples usually fall into one of two extremes.

On the positive side, we carry in our mind's eye a picture of evangelism that's based on highly effective pastors and teachers we've known, seen on stage, or watched on television or online. They are confident and articulate in talking about their faith. These people seem to know more than we do, are more accomplished than we are, or have skills that we don't have. We could never do what they do!

On the negative side, we harbor images of individuals who lack the skills to be effective and yet foist themselves on others just the same. They might be socially awkward, spiritually overbearing, or simply unable to clearly articulate what they're trying to explain. We don't want to be like them!

Do you see why these polar opposites put us off? We categorize evangelism as an activity for one of two kinds of Christ followers: Superstar Christians who have the skills needed to share the gospel effectively, or Offbeat Believers who lack those skills but do it anyway!

It's no wonder that many of us decide that outreach isn't

for us. The vast majority of believers end up in "evangelistic no-man's land," thinking *somebody* ought to be spreading the Good News—but that somebody isn't going to be *them*. Unfortunately, studies bear this out. A recent *LifeWay Research* publication reports, for example, that less than half of the churchgoers they surveyed (45 percent) had shared information on how to become a Christian with someone in the prior six months.[1]

The good news about the Good News is that we can reverse those trends by learning to authentically be ourselves while sharing Jesus with others. There are a variety of natural approaches we can take to reach the people around us—things we can say and do that fit our own God-given personalities. Specifically, I think you'll be encouraged by the five *Contagious Faith Styles* we'll explore in the chapters that follow.

It's liberating to realize that God knew what he was doing when he made you. *Your* personality is on purpose. You don't need to feel bad for not looking, acting, or talking like some other Christian. God wants to use you *as you*—as he equips and stretches you to reach out to others in your own uniquely effective way.

In fact, he has designed all of us to be missionaries within our own circle of friends. Think about this: the reason they are your friends is because they relate to people like you. That's right; friendship is voluntary. These people want to know you because you're their kind of person. That means that nobody—not me, not your pastor, not the most persuasive evangelist on television or social media—can relate to them the way that you can.

No wonder Paul said, "We are therefore Christ's ambassadors, as though God were making his appeal through us" (2 Corinthians 5:20). An effective ambassador is one who knows the language and culture of the people to whom he or she is sent. Well, that's you—nobody knows your family and friends the way you do. Nobody speaks their language, or relates to their culture, or is connected to their past, like you.

You can be that spiritual ambassador. *You* can be a God-appointed missionary, sent at least initially to reach the people you know best. Now you just need to get prepared. You need to find your natural niche for spiritually influencing others. You'll also want to hone a few *Key Skills* on how to tell them about your faith. Those are the things we're going to spend the bulk of this book doing—together.

Are you ready to get started?

A Contagious Vision

For my part, I soon learned what you might already know: *God has a sense of humor!*

Why do I say that? Because less than a year after thinking I'd walked away from being involved in evangelism, I was hired to be the first director of evangelism at what was rapidly becoming one of the most-attended churches in the United States, an innovative and influential congregation in Chicago that a leading global missiologist declared to be the most evangelistic church in North America.

Ironically, I was thrust into the middle of an outwardly focused movement, leading the charge to find new strategies to equip Christians to tell others about Christ and to get the gospel to countless outsiders who needed to know the Savior. I found a fresh passion for reaching people in ways that fit my God-given personality. And I began developing a vision for helping other

Christians find natural approaches to reaching people in their own lives, as well as helping them learn the skills they need to do so effectively.

As I stepped into my new role, I immediately began to write a training course designed to liberate the people in our own congregation. Along with my ministry partner and best buddy Lee Strobel (who would later pen *The Case for Christ* and many other bestselling books), I developed a pilot course that we taught month after month to new groups of people at the church, with the goal of helping every member share their faith effectively.

Then, after several years of refining those materials, we reshaped them so they could be used in other congregations and ministries around the world. When we finally published the training, we called it the *Becoming a Contagious Christian* course, and I coauthored a bestselling book by the same title.[2] The results astounded us over the years that followed. The course has been translated into more than twenty languages and has equipped nearly two million people around the world to share their faith in natural ways.

By God's grace, countless individuals have been reached through those who've been inspired and trained through these materials. I know men who were able to reach their wives, and women who reached their husbands and children. One close friend reached her dad soon before he died, and then she helped encourage and coach another woman who led both of her parents to Christ! There have been workers who have had a spiritual influence on their bosses. Many people's neighbors have been impacted for eternity. Students' lives have been transformed by the gospel. We've even seen a number of church attenders in our courses over the years come to realize that they'd never put their trust in Jesus personally, and then make the decision to receive him right then and there. I thank God for the ways he has worked through all of this—especially considering how much of it initially flowed out of my own awkward and uncomfortable experiences.

Looking Forward

But I believe we're just getting started! I've taken what I've learned in the years since then—along with some of the classic wisdom of the original materials—and put it into the *Contagious Faith* book you're reading, as well as the new *Contagious Faith* video training course that flows out of it. We're also spreading the training through online classes offered through our Lee Strobel Center for Evangelism and Applied Apologetics at Colorado Christian University. I hope you'll consider taking a class or two—or perhaps earning a certificate or an accredited undergraduate or master's degree—through this exciting new program.[3]

My sincere prayer is that this book will prepare you to share your faith in ways that really fit you—whether your main approach turns out to be the *Friendship-Building, Selfless-Serving, Story-Sharing, Reason-Giving,* or *Truth-Telling Contagious Faith Style*—or most likely a combination of several of them.

Also, I hope you'll consider using the *Contagious Faith* training course to deepen your own confidence in sharing Christ, and to help equip your small group, your class at church, or even your entire congregation with the approaches and skills needed to reach friends and family members with the gospel.

I believe that together we can discover new ways to approach evangelism, and then be unleashed to spiritually impact the lives of the people around us—for eternity.

THE FIVE CONTAGIOUS
FAITH STYLES

In the next five chapters, we're going to explore the five *Contagious Faith Styles*. We'll look at current examples of each of them, people who used these approaches in the New Testament, and situations where Jesus himself employed each of the styles. Then we'll unpack *Key Skills* that will help you become increasingly effective at communicating your faith.

As you go through these chapters, you'll be able to identify which style most naturally fits you. But I encourage you to be sure to read all five chapters, even if you think you already know which of these is your primary approach.

Why? You might be surprised to find you relate well to several of the styles we discuss, and you'll want to draw from elements of each of those in a combination that best fits you. And even if a particular approach doesn't seem to fit you, you'll probably think of other believers in your circle who do match with it. This can help you know how to best partner with them to reach your family and friends, as well as theirs.

Additionally, the *Key Skills* listed in the second part of each of these five chapters are essential for *all* of us—regardless of which style is our main one.

Now, you might be thinking that we should be less concerned about our own approach and much more about what the other person needs from us. And there's some truth in that. Paul did say that we need to "become all things to all people," so that by all possible means we might reach some of them with the gospel (1 Corinthians 9:19–23).

So, yes, we need to flex as much as possible to relate to people we're trying to reach. But that doesn't negate the fact that we still have certain personal parameters within which we'll generally be most effective. In other words, there will be certain people and situations we're better suited for than others. Once we understand what those are, we'll be wise to try to operate in those arenas as much as possible. And when we need to stretch beyond them, we may want to supplement our own efforts with those of another Christian whose natural style is better suited to the specific needs at hand.

It's much like the topic of spiritual gifts. While we should be ready and willing to serve wherever God leads us, we'll usually be most fruitful—and more fulfilled—when we're serving in areas that fit our natural, God-given areas of giftedness. And because the Holy Spirit knows this (and designed it that way), he'll most often lead us to serve in ways that are consistent with who he made us to be.

One last preliminary. It was the discovery of which styles were *not* mine, as well as which one *is*, that liberated me to get back on the playing field in reaching others for Christ. Finding your own natural approach will likely be liberating for you as well—but so will understanding various styles that don't particularly reflect your personality.

So, read on with an open heart and a prayerful attitude, asking God to show you which approaches will best fit you as well as the people he's calling you to reach.

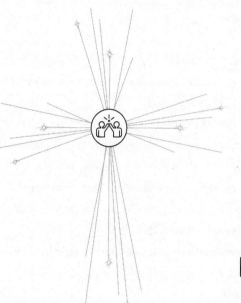

CHAPTER 3

STYLE #1:

FRIENDSHIP-BUILDING

"I have called you friends, for everything that I
learned from my Father I have made known to
you."

—JESUS, IN JOHN 15:15

Heidi and I had just moved into our new home in the woods of
Colorado when we were invited to our first "Flamingo Party."
What's that, you ask? It's when our neighbors gather on Friday
nights during the summer. The host home shifts each week, and
you know where the party is happening by looking for the gaudy
pink plastic birds by the side of a driveway. Find the flamingos,
and you've found the party.

We felt this was an answer to our prayers. God was opening
doors of relationship and influence with our neighbors. These
kinds of opportunities especially fit Heidi, who is socially outgoing and unafraid to engage new people in personal conversations.

At our inaugural flamingo party, we met Kathy. She was fun and gregarious, and her quieter fiancé, Don, seemed like a great guy as well. We all hit it off immediately.

In the days and weeks following that initial meeting, Heidi and Kathy began to connect with each other on social media. But soon it became clear that they were spiritually miles apart. Despite those differences, their friendship gradually deepened. And as we sensed a growing openness in Kathy, we began praying for God to work in both her and Don's life.

Heidi and Kathy's conversations became increasingly focused on spiritual matters. Kathy was always full of questions—which I sometimes helped to address.

Everything culminated one autumn day when Kathy told Heidi she wanted to bring over a new apple dessert—and to ask us a few more questions. As it turned out, the dessert was delicious, but the conversation was even better.

After we'd discussed several spiritual topics that Kathy raised, I asked if I could draw a picture that sums up the central message of Christianity. She was interested, so I drew my version of the Bridge Illustration—which demonstrates humanity's separation from God because of sin—and soon Kathy's tears began to flow. She was a ready learner, and before I'd even finished the drawing and explanation, Kathy got impatient and said, "I get it: God's over on that side and I'm still on this side. Tell me how to get over there!"

Kathy was ready! Through sobs of repentance and joy, she held Heidi's and my hands and prayed to ask Jesus to forgive her sins and lead her life. The date was October 19, 2011—Kathy's spiritual birthday—and she has never been the same.[1]

I've seen God use Heidi's natural relational approach in

similar ways many times over the years—including, as I've described, during our outreach tour of duty in England. And Kathy, too, has become a bold and joy-filled witness for Christ in our neighborhood, in her family and at work, and wherever she goes. It has been a thrill for us to see how God has worked in and through her since that day. And more than that, it's been fun to see that, like Heidi, Kathy is now an active model of the *Friendship-Building Contagious Faith Style*.

The Friendship-Building Contagious Faith Style

Friendship-Builders are people-people. They love spending time with friends while also making new ones. They have warm personalities. They enjoy nothing more than hanging out with interesting people, sharing good coffee, tea, or food together, and engaging with them in lively conversations.

These folks like to extend hospitality to others. They're generally not cause-driven or issue-oriented. Rather, they are relationship-oriented, with their natural focus being on individuals and their needs.

Some are extroverted and like to be with friends in larger groups. Others are introverted, preferring to be with individuals or in smaller gatherings. But they all enjoy being with people and want to spend time with them.

Perhaps this is your primary style. Don't be intimidated by the evangelistic successes of Heidi or the other examples I'll offer below. Most were a bit hesitant (or *very* hesitant) in the beginning. But they took baby steps and found that Jesus was serious when he said if we'd obey his command to share the Good News, then he'd be there to support and guide us. "And surely I am with you always, to the very end of the age" he promised (Matthew 28:20). They have discovered—*as you will*—that God's Spirit was with them and using them through their relational efforts.

Friendship-Building in Our Culture

This approach is vitally important in our society today. As you're probably aware, many people are jaded toward the church, toward Christians, and even toward God. A lot of them have had bad religious experiences in the past, so they can be resistant to our invitations to special events or services at our churches or fellowship groups.

But while they may seem closed spiritually, they're usually open relationally. Whether they know it or not, they are still created in the image of a relational God who has enjoyed loving friendships within the Trinity for all of eternity. No wonder we all crave relational connections and no surprise we hurt so badly when those are torn apart. Our need for deep personal connectedness is woven into the very fabric of what it means to be human.

People need people, and friends listen to friends. Just think of who *you* turn to when you're going through a hard time or need someone to speak into your life. Probably not some religious person who shows up at your door or sends you an unsolicited email. No, we naturally want to talk to someone we know and trust—and who we're confident will have our best interests at heart. In other words, we want to turn to a real friend.

Likewise, when we lovingly express a *Friendship-Building* approach with the folks around us, they're going to be drawn to it. They may say to themselves, *I'm not so sure about this gal's religion, but I sure like being around her!* Or, *I don't think I agree with this guy's beliefs, but I appreciate the way he treats me and the team at work.* God can use your relationships with these people to gradually open them up to a relationship with him.

Matthew: Tax Collector-Turned-Evangelist

For a biblical example of this approach, we can look to Jesus's disciple Matthew, who used a *Friendship-Building* style to reach out to his former tax-collecting coworkers. But before he discovered that style, it's easy to imagine him musing, *I'm not really articulate or super knowledgeable about biblical matters like some of the other guys in our newly formed discipleship group. And I'm certainly no public speaker. About all I know how to do is throw a party.*

Then a lightbulb goes on. *Wait a minute—that's what I'll do. I'll throw a party, but it will be a different kind of party—a party with a purpose!* And so we read in Luke 5:29 that Matthew, mentioned by his other name, Levi, "held a great banquet for Jesus at his house, and a large crowd of tax collectors and others were eating with them."

In effect, Matthew created an atmosphere where he, Jesus, and the other disciples could enjoy a meal and socialize with a bunch of Matthew's buddies—people he loved, but who believed and lived very differently than he now did. It was a custom-made *friendship-building* environment. He used hospitality to build on their common interests in food and fellowship, undoubtedly with the hope of starting spiritual conversations and having a contagious effect on these former colleagues whom he cared so much about.

His plan came together beautifully, with a houseful of his

friends gathering with Jesus and the other disciples. Wouldn't you have enjoyed sitting in the corner and hearing some of the dialogue that night?

All seemed to be going well until some of the nearby religious leaders got wind of what was happening. We're told in Luke 5:30 that they complained to the disciples, "Why do you eat and drink with tax collectors and sinners?" You see, they were limited by their separatist mindset, which told them they needed to stay apart from anyone who was not from their religious tribe. They believed that they would be spiritually stained by rubbing shoulders with such unsavory people, so they worked hard at keeping a safe distance away from them—much like some Christians do today.

Now, don't get me wrong. There are some dangers in hanging around with people who oppose your beliefs or values. It's for good reason that Paul warned us in 1 Corinthians 15:33, "Do not be misled: 'Bad company corrupts good character'"—though that was mostly a caution against associating with those who deny essential teachings of the faith (in their case, the resurrection of Jesus).

On the other hand, it was Jesus who challenged his disciples to *go into* the world with the goal of making more disciples (Matthew 28:18–20). He also prayed to the Father for them—and us—saying, "My prayer is not that you take them out of the world but that you protect them from the evil one. They are not of the world, even as I am not of it" (John 17:15–16). It's from this passage that many have deduced the phrase that, as Jesus's followers, we are to be "*in* the world, but not *of* the world." Also, Jesus added this to his prayer a couple verses later: "As you sent me into the world, I have sent them into the world" (verse 18).

So not only is it permissible for us to rub shoulders with people outside of God's family—it's *mandated* by Jesus that we do so. Still, this comes with inherent dangers. "I am sending you out like sheep among wolves," Jesus explained. "Therefore be as shrewd as snakes and as innocent as doves" (Matthew 10:16).

Putting all of this together, here's the biblical principle: We should spend time with the people God sent us to reach, but only as long as we remain the dominant spiritual influence in the relationship. If we sense the balance starting to shift in the other direction—where their influence is causing us to slip in our beliefs or behavior—then we need to pull back a bit, shore up our spiritual defenses, and finally reenter the situation when we are again ready to be a positive influence for Christ.

Going back to Matthew's party, it's revealing to see how Jesus responded to the challenge from the Pharisees about socializing with spiritual outsiders. Jesus said to them in Luke 5:31–32: "It is not the healthy who need a doctor, but the sick. I have not come to call the righteous, but sinners to repentance." Jesus was simply restating his purpose for coming to live among us in the first place: "For the Son of Man came to seek and to save the lost" (Luke 19:10).

Jesus: Friend of Sinners

Jesus himself often used a *Friendship-Building* approach to reach people. He got up close to the crowds. He also singled out individuals to talk with, sometimes to answer their questions and other times to ask *them* questions. He walked, talked, and ate with those he wanted to influence.

As a result, Jesus not only *risked* his reputation—he *ruined* it. Why do I say this? Because, as he explained, "The Son of Man came eating and drinking, and you say, 'Here is a glutton and a drunkard, a friend of tax collectors and sinners'" (Luke 7:34). His opponents meant this as an insult, but Jesus was undaunted. He truly was a friend of sinners, and he didn't care what the religious leaders thought about it.

One place we see Jesus using this relational style is in Luke 19, when he was traveling through Jericho. As he walked along, he noticed a guy named Zacchaeus—who also happened to be a tax collector—up in a sycamore-fig tree, trying to get a closer glimpse of him. Suddenly Jesus looked up at him and said, "Zacchaeus, come down immediately. I must stay at your house today" (verse 5).

You have to love what Jesus did! He didn't have a house of his own to invite this man to, and apparently there were no coffee shops nearby where they could meet. So instead Jesus invited himself to Zacchaeus's house—and Zacchaeus gladly accepted the self-summons.

The result? After spending time eating and talking, Zacchaeus suddenly stood up and demonstrated his change of heart that had resulted from getting to know Jesus. He announced: "Look, Lord! Here and now I give half of my possessions to the poor, and if I have cheated anybody out of anything, I will pay back four times the amount" (verse 8).

Jesus joyfully responded, "Today salvation has come to this house, because this man, too, is a son of Abraham." And it was here that Jesus added the declaration of his mission that we mentioned earlier: "For the Son of Man came to seek and to save the lost" (verses 9–10).

When I was in church growing up, we often sang the song, "Jesus! What a Friend for Sinners!" How true its words are still today:

> *Hallelujah! What a Savior!*
> *Hallelujah! What a friend!*
> *Saving, helping, keeping, loving,*
> *He is with me to the end.*

I'm thankful to know that Jesus is not just a friend to sinners like you and me, but he also wants to be a friend to all the other spiritual rule-breakers we know.

KEY SKILLS FOR EVERY CHRISTIAN

Whether or not the *Friendship-Building* style is your primary approach, here are three *Key Skills* regarding relationships that every one of us as believers should put into practice.

1. Start and Strengthen Relationships

The apostle Paul tells us in Colossians 4:5: "Be wise in the way you act toward outsiders; make the most of every opportunity." For most of us, the primary way we'll be able to share our faith with "outsiders" is relational. Yet studies show that the majority of us lose most of our non-Christian friends within a few years of coming to faith in Christ. It seems to happen naturally as we get more and more involved in our church and Christian activities. But if we're going to reach our world with the gospel, then this trend *must* change.

We need to think and act more like Jesus's disciple Matthew, and like Jesus himself, who lovingly reached out to the people around them in spite of spiritual or cultural differences with them. But where should we begin? There are three primary arenas: *Current Friendships*, *Lapsed Friendships*, and *New Friendships*.

Deepen Current Friendships

We tend to think it's more praiseworthy to start from scratch with strangers and then somehow take them all the way to the point of putting their trust in Christ. You might be able to do that at some point, but to begin let's follow Matthew's example when he reached out to the guys he knew from work.

We said earlier that *friends listen to friends*. So, the most natural place to start is with people we currently know. They already trust us. They are interested in our lives, just as we're interested in theirs. And they may already be curious about what makes us tick spiritually—especially if they knew us both before and after we put our faith in Jesus. Even though they might not know how to talk about it, they're watching our actions and wondering what motivates us.

The key is to simply find ways to get around them more often—including, at some point, in more private settings where you can have conversations about personal matters. That could include doing what Matthew did by opening your home to those inside and outside the faith. You might invite them for a meal, a party, or a relaxed dessert by the fireplace. The gathering could be built around a natural event like a birthday, a child's graduation, or a holiday. It might be to watch a sporting event that you know your friends or relatives would enjoy seeing together.

Such gatherings can be very simple—like telling the neighbors you'd enjoy having them come over on Friday night to help you try out a new recipe or break in a new grill. Or they can be more detailed, like having a neighborhood block party, a catered banquet at your home, or a sports night for everyone's kids. There's no formula. It's just a matter of getting folks together around a common interest or need, and then finding ways to encourage discussion.

We can also deepen relationships with people we already know by giving some forethought to upcoming times together. For example, if a family reunion or holiday gathering is coming up, prayerfully consider who you should try to get alone with during that time. Then send them a note that says, "I'm looking forward to seeing you soon—but while you're in town I'd love it if we could get away and catch up a bit. Maybe we should go to our old favorite café for breakfast." Most relatives will be happy to spend some focused time together, and it can become a great setting for a deeper conversation.

It can also be a bit more spontaneous, like asking someone after a family meal if they'd like to go for a stroll, or to hang out by the fire pit after others go to bed. Or you can take a similar approach with a work colleague during a break time or lunch hour. See if they'd like to walk a couple of blocks and try out the new coffee shop, or just get a little fresh air after a long team meeting. Or offer to go running together, shopping at a mall, fishing at a pond, studying for a test, or golfing on a new course. Be creative, and tailor your efforts to the interests of the person with whom you want to go deeper.

Also, we all tend to be busy, so it's helpful to consider what you're already going to do anyway—and then invite the person to join you in those activities. Are you planning to go for a bike ride or a hike, or to the gym, or to the park with the family? It doesn't take much more time or energy to ask others to join you, but it could end up making a world of difference in their lives.

Of course, pray for wisdom and open doors as you try to get closer to the person, so you influence them for Christ. Again, those are prayers God loves to answer!

Renew Lapsed Friendships

We all have people from our past we genuinely liked and intended to stay close to, but for no particular reason we grew apart from them. Maybe they moved to another city after graduation or a promotion at work. This reality provides an opportunity for us, because friends from the past are naturally curious to know "whatever happened" to you.

If you'll make the effort to reconnect, you'll find that they are delighted to hear your voice and anxious to find out where you live, what you're doing now, whether you have a family, and generally "what's new in your life."

This can open the door to renewed friendships and a chance to talk about what's new in your life *spiritually*— and what that might mean to them as well.

Start New Friendships

In addition, we have almost endless opportunities to form friendships with people we don't yet know—like Jesus did with Zacchaeus. But who are these people, and how can we best meet them?

First, you can take many of the examples given above and expand them to include new people. If you're going to arrange a meal with a relative around the holidays, does he or she have a new friend you could include? Or if you're going to have a gathering at your house, invite the two or three people who recently moved into your neighborhood. Or you could reach out to the new employee at work who might have some common interests with you and your friends.

Or what about people you naturally encounter throughout your week? The guy at the gas station, the lady who delivers the mail, the person who cuts your hair, the babysitter or tutor, the man who fixes your car or works in your yard, the new neighbor you see walking the dog, the barista at the coffee shop, or the waiter at the bistro. All of these can turn into chances to have a spiritual influence *if* we extend ourselves relationally.

I'm often amazed, for example, to see how a friend of mine is able to get to know waiters or waitresses. I often joke that he's the master of "restaurant outreach." How does he do it? Well, he finds a place he likes and then he goes back there often, sitting in the same section so he'll be served by the same waiter or waitress. Before you know it, he has learned their name, their spouse's name, and a little about their life. Soon he's praying for their needs, sharing a book with them, inviting them to church, or urging them to get in a small group where they can ask questions. Often these folks end up taking significant steps spiritually—and sometimes they end up putting their trust in Christ.

These are things we all can do, but we need to pray for the Holy Spirit to give us eyes to recognize the opportunities around us, and then to give us the wisdom and courage to go through the doors he opens for us.

2. Initiate Spiritual Conversations

We've looked at ways to get closer to people who are far from God, but in order to have a spiritual influence we're going to need to initiate conversations about him. And I'd recommend doing so sooner rather than later. Why? Because the longer we wait, the harder it gets. I think this stems from our intuitive sense that something that's really important can't be withheld too long. And if we wait several years to talk to a neighbor or classmate about Jesus, their response might be, "If it's so important, why am I just hearing about it now?"

The best way to prevent this is to drop spiritual hints as early in the relationship as possible. This can be done by casually referring to something you're doing with your youth group, or with your family at church, or by mentioning something you learned recently in a sermon or from reading the Bible or a Christian book. Or I often talk about some new Christian music I've been listening to.

These are things they might pick up on and ask more about—or they can just let them slide and move on to another topic. Either way, you've planted spiritual seeds. A week, month, or maybe even a year or two later they might be more open to talking about it. When that happens, your candor has already paved the way for them to discuss spiritual matters with you.

One way or another, a discussion will be needed. It's not enough to just live out our faith in front of people. We need to put our beliefs into words. As Paul asked, "How can they believe in him if they have never heard about him? And how can they hear about him unless someone tells them?" (Romans 10:14 NLT). So, since words are necessary, how can we get the conversation started? Let's discuss a few ideas.

Bridge from Standard Topics to Spiritual Ones

First, one of the most natural things we can do is move the conversation from everyday topics to spiritual ones. This is something that's easy to learn, though you don't want to do it all the time. Rather, ask God for wisdom about when and where to turn discussions to faith-related matters, and pray that he'll prepare the person ahead of time. Here are some examples.

If your friend is talking about his favorite sports team, you can bring up an example of a player you know to be a committed Christian. "I really enjoy that team, too," you could say. "And I found it interesting hearing the pitcher talk about how God helped him overcome his injury and play his best game. Did you catch that interview?"

Or you're discussing music, and you can mention a musician whose life has been changed through Christ, or you could talk about one of his or her songs that raises issues that have spiritual overtones.

Or if the topic of history, science, or psychology comes up, you can mention how something you read recently in that area reinforced your faith in God or your confidence in the Bible. For example, evidence about the beginning of the universe or the complexity of creation can easily be utilized to talk about the Creator behind those phenomena.

Sometimes I reference the beauty or wonder of nature. For example, I'll comment on a breathtaking sunset or a stunning view of the mountains, and say something like, "There must be quite an Artist behind that gorgeous artwork, don't you think?" Now, they might believe nature can account for everything we see. That's okay. Remember that our goal at this point is to simply get the conversation started—not to necessarily have them agree with what we say. And if they do offer alternative explanations, it's pretty easy to ask them questions about their beliefs to keep the discussion going . . . but that's the topic of the next section.

Ask Curiosity Questions

Curiosity questions are a natural way to initiate or extend a spiritual conversation. You could say something like, "I'm curious, do you ever think about spiritual matters?"

Or, "What is your religious background? Is it something you still practice today?" Or when Christmas or Easter is coming, you can say, "I was wondering, does your family have any traditions related to the holiday? Or do you attend any special services?" If they don't, you could ask what they were taught growing up. If they've since departed from those beliefs, you can ask them why.

Or you can ask about specific topics related to the holidays. For example, you might mention that there are some pretty big claims related to Easter and ask them if they believe Jesus really rose from the dead. If they say they doubt it—or that such things are impossible— you might say, "That's interesting. The early reports said that the tomb was empty. What do you think might have happened to Jesus's body?"

Again, remember that our aim is not to necessarily find agreement with them at this point, but to get them talking about whatever they believe and why. This can lead to ongoing conversations and a deepening friendship. Don't feel that you need to have ready responses to the opinions they raise. Instead, you can make it a matter to explore together on a quest for greater understanding—all in the context of the relationship.

Turn Invitations into Conversations

Another way to initiate spiritual conversations is to simply invite your friend to an event or service at your church—or perhaps a discussion group where questions are explored at a deeper level. Or it could just be a Christian concert, movie, or seminar.

Surveys indicate as many as one third of our friends will be interested enough to attend with us. That's really good news—but here's more good news: of the two thirds who will decline the invitation, many will still be open to discussions flowing out of it. They may say something like, "I don't think I'm ready to visit a church, but if you'd ever like to grab a drink and talk about this stuff, I'd be willing to do that." Well, that's a great response and an important opportunity—so be sure to take them up on it.

But even if they don't turn your invitation into a conversation, it's pretty easy for *you* to do so. For example, if they turn you down strongly, saying, "No thanks—I have absolutely no interest in anything related to organized religion," then you can quip with a twinkle in your eye, "Well, our church is not very organized at all—so I think you might like it!" Or you can get more serious, and say, "It sounds like you've had some negative experiences with religious organizations. Could I ask what happened?"

Regardless of how people respond to your invitations to strategic events, these moments can turn into opportunities for further conversation. But while we're on the topic of inviting friends to events, how can we do so effectively? That's what we'll discuss next.

3. Invite Friends into Life-Changing Environments

Don't underestimate the potential of bringing your friends to a church service or spiritual discussion group.

It's not just a matter of what they'll hear in the sermon or conversation, but it's also the experience of sitting among committed believers who are singing heartfelt songs of worship to the heavenly Father who made us. It's seeing us pray to the Savior who paid the penalty for our sins. It's feeling the presence of the Holy Spirit and sensing that he is touching their heart or pricking their conscience—all the while awakening them to their need for salvation.

It's interesting to remember that the author Lee Strobel, who was an atheist, came to faith because, first, his agnostic wife Leslie was invited by a friend to a church service. This led to Leslie's commitment to Christ, and then to her own subsequent invitations to Lee to come to that same church. He finally did, and that helped spawn his own spiritual journey that eventually led him to trust in Jesus as well.[2]

So how can we best invite our friends and family to strategic spiritual gatherings? Here are three ideas.

Tailor Invitations to Interests and Needs

Try to invite friends to events that will address their particular questions, meet the needs they're concerned about, or just be something you think they'd enjoy. This might be as simple as inviting neighbors to your church when your pastor will be speaking on a topic of concern to them—like what the Bible says about how to have a better marriage or build a stronger family. Or it could be a matter of asking them to join you for a Christian concert that will feature the kinds of music they most enjoy (and maybe giving them a recording or sending them a link to a video so they can check out the group ahead of time).

Perhaps your friend has been asking challenging spiritual questions, and there's a speaker coming to your church to give a talk on the evidence for Christianity, followed by an open-mic question-and-answer session. Or maybe you could ask if your friend would like to attend a small group for spiritually curious people when you or your church begins offering ministry opportunities like that.

Your invitation will be attractive if you tailor it to their interests, questions, or concerns. That, combined with your friendship and the influence of the Holy Spirit, can all work together to be a highly effective approach in leading them to the Savior.

Provide Printed Information

It's good to invite your friend to a strategic event, but you'll greatly increase your odds of getting them there if you put something printed in their hands. This should include all the information they need regarding when and where it is, how to park, where to register, and so forth. Don't underestimate how intimidating it can be for someone who hasn't been to church for years—or who has never attended before—to walk through the doors for the first time. Eliminating confusion about the details will go a long way toward easing their concerns.

Bring Your Friend with You

By far, the best way to get your friends to actually show up is to *bring them with you*. So, after explaining what the event is and why you think they'd enjoy it, and after giving them printed information, offer to pick them up and go together.

Better yet, if there's a cost for the event, tell them you'll buy their ticket and even take them out for a meal or coffee afterward. That way they'll see that you're not just trying to get them to do something; you're joining them in it as a friend. Your small investment of time and resources might just lead them into a process that changes, well, their entire life's trajectory!

Cautions Concerning the *Friendship-Building* Style

As we'll see with all five of the *Contagious Faith Styles*, there are some cautions we need to beware of related to the *Friendship-Building* approach.

Stay Genuine

First, make sure your relational efforts are genuine, and that you present yourself and your intentions honestly and authentically. No one wants to be manipulated. Don't feign a faux friendship in order to try move someone toward Christ. That will backfire, and it won't properly represent our Savior, who was always forthright with others.

Rather, extend yourself as a real friend as it seems

appropriate—but make sure you aren't attaching any strings or conditions to the relationship. Show genuine love for the person whether they agree with you or not. And don't hide the fact that part of how you love people is by telling them the truth about God and his gracious offer of forgiveness and salvation. I'm not saying you need to announce this whenever you meet people, but if you're open about who you are and what you believe, and about your excitement to help others meet and follow the Savior, it will keep them from thinking you have a hidden agenda. You want to be a real friend *and* you want to introduce them to the greatest Friend they could ever know.

Establish Boundaries

Avoid misunderstandings with members of the opposite gender. Some say that in our promiscuous times it's too risky to try sharing Jesus with the other sex. I understand that concern, but I disagree with the conclusion.

Remember that Jesus reached out to the Samaritan woman in John 4—commonly known as "the woman at the well." But he was wise in how he did this, talking to her in broad daylight and in a public place. The result? Not only did he lead this precious woman to trust in him, but through her, many of her friends were also reached, and it helped form the first fellowship of Jesus-followers in her little town in Samaria.

Similarly, you may have noticed that a number of the stories I've already told involved me sharing my faith with women. I'm thankful God has used me to spiritually influence both men and women, but I've learned to establish some parameters to try to prevent being misunderstood. This has included having honest conversations along the way—especially when I was single—in which I explained that my interactions with them were motivated by a spiritual concern—*not* a romantic interest. I remember one of them responding, "Oh, thanks for explaining . . . I wasn't sure what to think!" I was glad I had cleared the air so we could continue the conversation without confusion.

Prioritize Truth

One more important caution for the *Friendship-Building* style: Beware of valuing friendship over truth. In other words, don't get so caught up in having a smooth relationship that you shrink back from sharing the gospel with your friend. Telling the person that they are a sinner who needs a Savior can create ripples in the relational pond—but if we really love them, then we must be willing to take that risk.

When you think about it, that's what real friendship demands: caring about the other person enough to tell them what they need to hear. If they are headed for disaster—especially in the spiritual realm—you might have to tell them some unpleasant truths in order to protect them from what's coming.

Even the well-known comedian and magician Penn Gillette, who is an outspoken atheist, agrees with this. He tells the story of a sincere Christian who took the risk of giving him a Bible after one of his shows. He defends that person by saying: "If you believe that there's a heaven and a hell . . . how much do you have to hate somebody to *not* proselytize? . . . I mean, if I believed, beyond the shadow of a doubt, that a truck was coming at you, and you didn't believe that truck was bearing down on you, there is a certain point where I tackle you. And this is more important than that."[3]

What a strong statement, especially coming from a non-believer: *How much do you have to hate someone* not *to warn them?*

The Bible reflects the same concern. According to Proverbs 27:5–6, "Better is open rebuke than hidden love. Wounds from a friend can be trusted, but an enemy multiplies kisses." Our goal is never to hurt someone, but like a good surgeon, we sometimes have to risk causing a little pain in order to help save a life. Except in this case, it's their *eternal* life!

The Extraordinary Impact of Building Friendships with Unbelievers

Julie was one of the shyest people I had ever met. Back in my early days of ministry in Chicago, she was so quiet and reserved that she would almost whisper when she talked to me. Yes, she was friendly—and she really did like people. But I'm pretty sure if you would have looked up the word *introvert* in the dictionary, you'd find a picture of Julie.

The good news, though, is that she was motivated to share the Good News with others. She would often meet with me to ask for ideas on how to reach out to her family members. She would read any articles or books I would recommend. She would look up things I'd suggest she research. And when I urged her to come to our evangelism seminar, she showed up for the class. In fact, Julie ended up taking those early renditions of our training course multiple times.

Gradually, Julie's confidence in talking about her faith began to grow. In her own reserved and quiet way, Julie built and deepened relationships with the people she hoped to spiritually influence. It wasn't long before she led her husband to Christ. Then her parents. Then her teenage daughters. Then a few nephews, and some of their friends. She even led a visitor at our church to trust in Jesus during a tour of the building. In fact, in one year's time, Julie led *fourteen people* to faith in Christ.

And you know what? Julie is *still* shy and introverted. She's exactly who God made her to be—and he delights to work through her to impact the lives of others. And she's a great example of how God can and often does use our efforts to build deeper friendships and to initiate richer conversations with the people in our lives.

Let me encourage you with a final thought for this chapter: *Your friends are more interested in spiritual matters than you think they are.* I know you might find that hard to believe, but it's true. People don't tend to let on how much they think about such things, but for many folks it's a frequent source of questions and concern. So, take a risk. Get up closer to them. Initiate spiritual conversations, ask questions, offer invitations—and often you'll be surprised at how positively people will respond.

And remember: the Holy Spirit is with you in this. He's guiding, empowering, and using you in ways that will make a lasting difference. Move ahead with confidence and discover what he wants to do through your efforts as you contagiously reach out to others for him.

God wants to do something amazing in and through your life. And, in the end, I think he is going to use you to spiritually impact the lives of others—in ways that will *never* end.

CHAPTER 4

STYLE #2:

SELFLESS-SERVING

"Let your light shine before others, that they may see your good deeds and glorify your Father in heaven."

—JESUS, IN MATTHEW 5:16

During Hurricane Harvey, the horrific 1,000-year storm that dropped a record 60 inches of rain on Houston and an estimated 33 trillion gallons of water over the southern United States, an elderly retiree named Morris and his wife were struggling. They were devastated when their home flooded and much of what they owned was damaged or destroyed.

In spite of being a successful lawyer and engineer for a large oil company, Morris didn't know where to turn. He was Jewish, but agnostic, so reaching out to God wasn't high on his list of options.

However, a church from the area sent a mother and her

teenage daughter, aptly named Grace, to serve them. They helped start the long process of cleaning things up, brought them meals, and even assisted in arranging for their damaged home to be repaired.

Morris was deeply impacted by the love of God shown by Grace and her mom. After it was all over, he was surprised—on top of everything else they had done—to receive a card in the mail from them. He opened it and said to his wife, "Look, they sent us a picture of Jesus. Why would they do that?" But his wife looked at the photograph and said, "That's not Jesus, Morris— that's a picture of *Grace!*"

Morris was sure he had seen the face of Jesus in that photo. That's how much the love of God, expressed through the sacrificial service of these two godly women, had influenced him. Because of the love they showed him, he became much more open to the idea of God and *his* love. He later attended a men's event at their church where a guest teacher was speaking on the evidence for Jesus's resurrection. This was something Morris had never heard about in his Jewish upbringing.

After the event, Morris told that teacher a bit about his journey and said he had a lot of questions. They met for a meal—and ended up talking for much of the afternoon. And just before Christmas of that same year, Morris received Christ as his forgiver and leader, and he was then baptized as a follower of Jesus, the Messiah.

All of this happened because a mother and daughter loved God enough to come and help Morris and his wife in the midst of a storm. Can you see the power and the potential in loving selfless service? It's a potency as old as the church itself.

The Selfless-Serving Contagious Faith Style

Those who fit the *Selfless-Serving* approach are naturally attuned to the needs of the people around them, and they find delight in meeting those needs. They usually work behind the scenes, and their efforts can often go unnoticed to everyone except the person who is being served. But because they are others-centered, they don't mind serving without a spotlight or any kind of fanfare to keep them motivated. They find joy in simply serving, and if that can be used by God to draw the person closer to him, that's all the better.

Many people today have put up a wall between themselves and God, the church, and Christians. Perhaps something happened in their lives that hardened them toward Christianity, or maybe the world has just beaten them up to the point that they don't trust anyone—God or his people included.

Regardless of the cause of their resistance, those who use the *Selfless-Serving* approach need to do whatever they can to try to win their trust, show them real love, and point them back to the Savior. They need to "become all things to all people so that by all possible means [they] might save some" (1 Corinthians 9:22). And I can't think of a better way to do that than to serve them in the name of Christ.

When we selflessly meet the needs of others, we demonstrate to them that they are valuable and loved—both by God and by us, his children—regardless of the barriers they've erected. In effect, we get behind the wall with them and, over time, help them tear it down, brick by brick. It may take a while, but our service can help them become more open spiritually, eventually leading them to trust in Jesus. As he put it in the Sermon on the Mount, "Let your light shine before others, that they may see your good deeds and glorify your Father in heaven" (Matthew 5:16).

Here's what's exciting: the *Selfless-Serving* style often reaches the hardest to reach people—those who may not be open at this point to a friendship or a spiritual conversation. When we sacrificially help them with their needs, this kind of Christlike service can soften the hardest of hearts and open the most closed of minds. Think about Morris. How do you think that he, with his Jewish upbringing, would have responded to a couple of Christians knocking at his door and trying to engage him in a conversation about Jesus? Or to a Jewish coworker who wanted to talk about the spiritual journey that led him to trust in the true Messiah?

My guess is that those approaches—which can be powerful in some contexts—might not have been nearly as effective as having a godly girl named Grace show up at his door, along with her mom, asking if they could help rescue and restore his flooded home. It's simply hard to resist someone who is setting aside their own concerns to help you with yours. This was as true in biblical times as it is today.

Tabitha Selflessly Serves People in Need

For a New Testament example of this approach, we can look to Tabitha, also called by her Greek name, Dorcas. Tabitha was a woman from Joppa who we read about in Acts 9. This account doesn't give us a lot of details, but it shows us that she was known in her village for lovingly serving people who were in need. Luke tells us in verse 36 that she "was always doing good and helping the poor," and he mentions in verse 39 the articles of clothing she had made for the widows of the town.

We might think of Tabitha as sort of a first-century Mother Teresa—someone who cared for people in ways that made heads turn heavenward. *There must be a God*, they'd say to themselves after seeing such tangible forms of compassion in action. *Just look at how lovingly his daughter serves so many of us!*

God too must have valued Tabitha and her selfless service. How do we know? We read in Acts 9:37 that she became sick and died, and it caused much sorrow in her community. So, what did God do? He sent his apostle, Peter, who was in the nearby town of Lydda, to go and pray over Tabitha's lifeless body, raise her to life, and put her back into service.

See how important the *Selfless-Serving* approach can be? Tabitha was helping people in vitally needed ways. But, in addition, she was undoubtedly influencing many of them spiritually, leading them to consider the Savior who motivated her to so tangibly love and care for those around her.

Son of Man, Servant to All

Jesus was the ultimate example of this approach. In Mark 10:43–45 he said to his followers, "Whoever wants to become great among you must be your servant, and whoever wants to be first must be slave of all. For even the Son of Man did not come to be served, but to serve."

How did Jesus serve them? In John 13 we read the account of the Last Supper, specifically how Jesus humbly assisted his disciples by washing their feet—a role usually filled by a servant in the house, not a respected religious teacher. His actions were so surprising that the disciples resisted at first, but Jesus insisted. He was serving them, but he was also teaching them an important lesson.

"I have set you an example that you should do as I have done for you," he said. "Very truly I tell you," he continued, "no servant is greater than his master, nor is a messenger greater than the one who sent him. Now that you know these things, you will be blessed if you do them" (verses 15–17).

Jesus's service was not limited to that example or to those in his immediate presence. Looking again at his words in Mark 10:45, he said, "The Son of Man did not come to be served, but to serve . . . *and to give his life as a ransom for many*" (emphasis mine).

Jesus was predicting his ultimate selfless act on behalf of all of humanity—on behalf of you and me—in laying down his life to die on the cross in order to pay for our sins, suffer our shame, and purchase our salvation. This was his very purpose in coming: to sacrifice *his* life in order to save *ours*.

KEY SKILLS FOR EVERY CHRISTIAN

Whether or not the *Selfless-Serving* style is your primary approach, here are three *Key Skills* that are important for all of us to put into practice. These can form a foundation of compassion that will help us extend God's love and truth to people in virtually any situation.

1. Nurture a Spirit of Empathy

In order to be motivated and effective in reaching out to others for Christ—and particularly to foster the right spirit behind the *Selfless-Serving* style—we must nurture the attribute of empathy. The Merriam-Webster dictionary defines *empathy* as "understanding, being aware of, being sensitive to, and vicariously experiencing the feelings, thoughts, and experience of another."[1]

This, unfortunately, is lacking in many of our lives. Without it, we end up preoccupying ourselves mostly with our own needs, plans, and futures, easily overlooking the problems, concerns, and destinies of the people around us. This is only encouraged by the spirit of our age, in which people are increasingly "lovers of themselves, lovers of money" (2 Timothy 3:2). These days, genuinely looking out for the needs of others is truly countercultural.

Against these tendencies, Jesus said we must love our neighbors as ourselves (Mark 12:31). Doing this requires recognizing and acting upon the kinds of concerns we have for ourselves, but instead doing so for the sake of others. Jesus's Golden Rule is built on this value: "In everything, do to others what you would have them do to you" (Matthew 7:12). He is telling us to consider the needs that *we* have, and then to project them onto *others* in order to serve them in ways that we'd like to be served. This is true empathy in action.

Paul echoed these thoughts when he admonished us in Philippians 2:3–4, "Do nothing out of selfish ambition or vain conceit. Rather, in humility value others above yourselves, not looking to your own interests but each of you to the interests of the others."

He went on to illustrate how Jesus modeled these

values for us. In Philippians 2:5–8 he says, "In your relationships with one another, have the same mindset as Christ Jesus: Who, being in very nature God, did not consider equality with God something to be used to his own advantage; rather, he made himself nothing by taking the very nature of a servant, being made in human likeness. And being found in appearance as a man, he humbled himself by becoming obedient to death—even death on a cross!"

So out of empathy for our hopeless spiritual situation, the Son of God gave up his heavenly perks and "humbled himself" to become not only our servant but also the sacrifice for our sins. No wonder the writer of Hebrews was able to say of Jesus (4:15–16), "For we do not have a high priest who is unable to *empathize* with our weaknesses, but we have one who has been tempted in every way, just as we are—yet he did not sin. Let us then approach God's throne of grace with confidence, so that we may receive mercy and find grace to help us in our time of need" (emphasis mine).

In every way, God set the example through Jesus of what empathy looks like, and the apostle Paul challenges us to "be imitators of God as dear children" (Ephesians 5:1 NKJV).

How can we do this? In part, by asking ourselves the classic question, "What would Jesus do?" whenever we see someone in need of help or encouragement. The more we can see people through his eyes, and then serve them with his spirit of empathy and concern, the more we'll be able to open them up to his love and truth as well.

2. Make Room for Divine Interruptions

In order to be effective in reaching out to others for Christ, we need to manage our schedules, as well as our attitudes, in the midst of *divine interruptions*. Here's what I wrote about this for the devotional book, *The Case for Christ Daily Moment of Truth*:

> "As Jesus and his disciples . . . were leaving the city, a blind man, Bartimaeus . . . was sitting by the roadside begging. When he heard that it was Jesus of Nazareth, he began to shout, 'Jesus, Son of David, have mercy on me!'" (Mark 10:46–47).
>
> Have you ever noticed that much of Jesus's ministry happened in the midst of interruptions? As he was "leaving the city," for instance, a blind man called out to him. It would have been easy for Jesus to say to his disciples, "Sorry, guys, it's not on the agenda. We have other obligations to fill, so tell him it'll have to wait."
>
> Can you imagine? Instead, Jesus asked the man what he wanted, and he ended up restoring the man's sight. All on his way out of town!
>
> In Acts 3 we read that "Peter and John were going up to the temple at the time of prayer" when a man who was lame asked them for money (verse 1). They could have decided prayer meetings were more important and kept on walking. Instead, they reached out to him, healed him, and changed his life forever.
>
> And in Acts 16 Paul was looking for a prayer

meeting down by a river. Apparently he never found it but instead "sat down and began to speak to the women who had gathered there" (verse 13). This led to one of those women, named Lydia, along with her entire household, trusting in Christ (verses 14–15).

See a pattern? No, we can't meet every need or stop every time someone wants to talk—and neither could Jesus and his followers. But like Jesus and these early Christian leaders, we need to stay open, always watching for divine interruptions that God might be opening up to us while we're on our way to do other things.[2]

Haven't you found this to be true? People who are in need almost never show up when we're all caught up with everything and just looking for someone to serve. No, it's generally at inopportune moments—times when we're already feeling overwhelmed with our own lives and concerns. I'm not sure if it's Murphy's Law or a divine test, but I think it's for this reason that God inspired the apostle Paul to write in Colossians 4:5–6, "Be wise in the way you act toward outsiders; make the most of every opportunity. Let your conversation be always full of grace, seasoned with salt, so that you may know how to answer everyone." Similarly, Paul told Timothy to "be prepared in season and out of season" (2 Timothy 4:2).

That means you should manage your life so that you can be open and watching for the divine interruptions God might bring your way this week, as he attracts people to you who need to be served in the name of

Christ. The situations might feel challenging—scratch that, they *will* feel challenging—but the impact of your response can be both exponential and eternal.

3. Develop Discernment about Who to Serve

There's one more essential skill we need to address: Knowing when to serve and when not to. Why is this so important? Because there will be an endless array of needs around you, and you'll never be able to meet them all—though you could die trying!

It's fascinating to see that the same Savior who was so open to divine interruptions was also willing to walk away (or sometimes *sail* away) from situations where there were still more people who needed to be healed, fed, taught, or encouraged. If even the incarnate Son of God had to pass on certain situations, then you and I will certainly need to do so as well.

I have a wise pastor friend, Kevin Harney, who recently wrote a book called, *No Is a Beautiful Word: Hope and Help for the Overcommitted and (Occasionally) Exhausted.* If that title alone brings tears to your eyes, then you should probably read it!

In the opening pages, Harney describes how he "discovered the beauty, the power, and the glory of a well-spoken and heartfelt no!"[3] This led him to become a happier and more productive person, freeing up enough time and energy for him to be able to start saying a more solid yes to things that really matter—like serving the needs of people God puts in his path.

The fact is that we live in a world that can quickly overwhelm us with busyness, daily demands, and sudden disasters. On top of all that, here I am, urging you to watch for ways to serve people around you. How can we do it all?

Simple answer: *We can't.*

That's why we need the wisdom of Scripture and the guidance of the Holy Spirit. God is able to lead us to say no to many opportunities so that we can say yes to the right ones, and then back up our yes with wholehearted love and action. Learning this skill, and discerning God's direction concerning who, where, and how long to serve, will enable us to help others in more strategic ways and therefore have a greater impact over the long haul.

Cautions Concerning the *Selfless-Serving* Style

As with the other styles, there are a few cautions worth considering.

Serve without Conditions

We need to make sure that when we commit to serving others, we don't do so in a conditional way. Our service needs to be motivated by love and care, with no strings attached. As soon as we start proportioning our willingness to help based on the other person's level of spiritual openness, they will feel they're being manipulated—and rightly so. If you read the John 13 passage carefully, you'll notice that Jesus washed the feet of *all* of his disciples, including Judas, who he knew would betray him later that very night. His service was not conditioned on how they were responding to his love and friendship. We need to follow his example.

Explain What Motivates You

We need to beware of the dangerous tendency to serve silently. People with this style are often less vocal, preferring to show their love in quiet but tangible ways. That's okay, but at some point it's important to let the person know that it's the love of Christ that motivates you. You can do this in ways that fit you, whether with a simple word, a written note, the gift of a Christian book, or maybe an invitation to your church or another Christian event.

Just don't leave them thinking you're simply genetically predisposed to being nice. Again, as Jesus said in Matthew 5:16, "Let your light shine before others, *that they may see your good deeds and glorify your Father in heaven*" (emphasis mine). But how will they know to glorify the Father unless we somehow direct their attention to him?

And remember Paul's challenge in Romans 10:14 (NLT), "And how can they believe in him if they have never heard about him? And how can they hear about him unless someone tells them?" We need to *tell* them. We must put the meaning behind our actions into words they can understand and respond to.

Some might say that if part of your motivation is to influence the person spiritually, then your motives are somehow misguided or inappropriate. I disagree. This needs to be a both/and. We should be driven to serve people because we genuinely care about them and their needs, *and* we should be motivated to point them to the Savior because we genuinely care about their soul and eternal destiny. These dual concerns compel us to the same kinds of loving activities.

Practice Patience

One more caution is in order. You're going to need patience. As I said earlier, your *Selfless-Serving* approach can reach the hardest-to-reach people—but that rarely happens quickly. Some of the barriers people have constructed to keep out God are well established and strong. There are people who have been so deeply hurt by the church or by religious people that they're going to be extra cautious. Helping someone in that situation take down their wall "brick by brick" can be a long and sometimes arduous process.

Don't expect rapid results, and resist getting frustrated. Just keep serving selflessly and consistently pray for the people you serve, knowing that God is working in and through you. He knows how, over time, to help them *"see your good deeds and glorify your Father in heaven."*

 ## The Extraordinary Impact of Selfless Serving

It was the middle of the pandemic. Nobody had seen anything like it before. People were becoming ill, rapidly declining, landing in the hospital, and often dying there. And the sickness was quickly spreading to others who had been around them.

What's worse, this novel virus was so little understood that when someone did get sick, their friends and family members were discouraged from even visiting them. This was based on the fear that they, too, would somehow contract the illness and end up on their own deathbed—perhaps next to the loved one they had visited.

How did this illness spread? Was it by simple touch? Was it in the air? Was it passed through bodily fluids? At the beginning no one really knew, so everyone was cautioned to play it safe and stay clear of anyone who might be infected. As a result, many who were ill were left to suffer in isolation, and they often spent their final days alone.

In the midst of this horrific situation a man named Roy contracted the disease. Soon, like so many others, he was languishing by himself, with almost none of his friends willing to take the risk of coming to see him. But a rare exception was Pat, a man Roy had gotten to know years earlier. Pat and his wife were committed Christians, and despite the highly publicized dangers of this disease, they felt compelled to visit Roy.

Throwing caution to the wind, they came to stand by Roy's bed. They were there to love, encourage, and serve him in any way they could—including, as prescribed in James 5:14, by anointing him with oil and praying for him.

Roy was moved by their love and concern, as well as by their willingness to sacrifice their own safety on his behalf. And although he wasn't known as a religious person, he was quite open to hearing what Pat Boone and his wife Shirley, as well as several other Christians who visited him around that time, shared about God's salvation.

In fact, it was through these visits and interactions that Roy Fitzgerald, who was much better known by his Hollywood screen name—Rock Hudson—prayed to receive Christ. Only a day or so later, this world-renowned actor died of the horrific pandemic—not Covid-19, but rather the pandemic of that era, HIV/AIDS.

"We all wept afterwards," Pat reported years later. And, based on Roy's receptivity and response to the gospel, Pat concluded, "he went to be with the Lord. AIDS had ruined his normal physical body, but now the Bible says we're given new bodies—eternal bodies. And now we believe that Roy . . . is there with the Lord and he'll welcome us when we come to our eternal habitations."[4]

The selfless actions of Pat, Shirley, and several other followers of Christ served to open this legendary actor to the God who loved him more than any of us ever could.

I'll say it one more time: Selflessly serving others will help us reach the hardest-to-reach people. The unlikely candidates for Christ. Even the most spiritually closed people will often open up to someone who they're convinced has their best interests in mind—the person who serves them from the heart and meets their genuine needs. Virtually no one will refuse that kind of tangible love when we offer it freely.

When people understand that our service is without expectation of anything in return, they will often grow curious and begin to ask questions. Serve with that goal in mind, because it's at this stage you can begin to point them to the people, places, and resources that will meet their spiritual needs and help them through their struggles.

What starts with the giving of tangible help can lead to the quenching of spiritual thirst. Acts of loving service can prompt decisions to follow the loving Savior.

Regardless of how the other person responds, God will be pleased with your selfless service done in the name of Jesus. I think he would say to you what Paul said to the believers in Corinth, in 1 Corinthians 15:58: *"Therefore, my dear brothers and sisters, stand firm. Let nothing move you. Always give yourselves fully to the work of the Lord, because you know that your labor in the Lord is not in vain."*

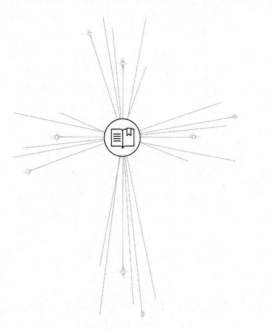

CHAPTER 5

STYLE #3:

STORY-SHARING

We proclaim to you what we have seen and
heard, so that you also may have fellowship with
us. And our fellowship is with the Father and
with his Son, Jesus Christ.

—1 JOHN 1:3

"I'm going to tell you a story. It's a true story. It's *my* story," said Lee Strobel to a large gathering at a church in southern California.

"It's a story that begins in atheism. I decided as a teenager that God does not, and cannot, exist. I thought God didn't create people, but people created God. Why? Because they were afraid of death, so they made up this idea of heaven to make themselves feel better about dying. I thought the mere concept of an all-loving, all-knowing, and all-powerful creator of the universe was crazy—and not worth my time to check out.

"Now, granted," he continued, "I tend to be a skeptical

person. My background is in journalism and law, so you can imagine when you put those two things together what kind of a jerk—I mean *skeptic*—you get! I was the legal editor of *The Chicago Tribune*, and we used to pride ourselves on our skepticism. We didn't want to accept anybody's word at face value. We always tried to get at least two sources to confirm a fact before we printed it in the newspaper. So, no kidding, we had a sign in our newsroom that said,

> **If your mother says she loves you . . . check it out!**

"How do you *know*? Maybe she's lying! Got any proof? Got any evidence?

"But that's okay—you want journalists to have a degree of skepticism. That's good. But the problem was that my skepticism bubbled over into *cynicism*, and it cemented me into my *atheism*. So, because I had no belief in God, I lacked a moral framework in my life. The way I looked at things was that if there is no God, if there is no heaven, if there is no hell, if there is no judgment, if there is no ultimate accountability, then the most logical way for me to live my life would be as a hedonist—someone who just pursued pleasure. And that's what I did. I lived a very immoral, drunken, profane, narcissistic, self-absorbed and, in a lot of ways, self-destructive kind of life. I had a lot of rage and anger . . ."[1]

Strobel continued, unpacking his testimony as the audience sat motionless in their seats, waiting for some kind of resolution to the spiritual tension they felt during the opening lines of his dramatic conversion story.

If you've read the bestselling book *The Case for Christ*,

or watched the movie by the same name, you know how his account unfolds. Lee's wife Leslie suddenly announced that she had become a Christian—which, to him at that time, was "the worst news possible." The first word to come to his mind, Lee explains, was *divorce*, because he felt like the victim of a classic bait-and-switch scheme, having signed up for life with one Leslie and suddenly being stuck with a different Leslie.

In fact, this marital jolt motivated Lee to do an intense investigation into the foundations of Leslie's newfound faith, in the hope that he could discredit it and, in the process, rescue his wife from the "cult" she had unwittingly joined.

"As far as I was concerned, the case was closed," Strobel wrote years later in the introduction to *The Case for Christ*. "There was enough proof for me to rest easy with the conclusion that the divinity of Jesus was nothing more than the fanciful invention of superstitious people. Or so I thought."[2]

Lee's quest for answers lasted for almost two years, but the deeper he looked the more unyielding the information became. Jesus said in Matthew 7:7–8, "Seek and you will find; knock and the door will be opened to you. For everyone who asks receives; the one who seeks finds; and to the one who knocks, the door will be opened." Jesus added in John 8:32, "You will know the truth, and the truth will set you free"—and that pretty well describes Lee's journey. What he had hoped would point *away* from the veracity of Leslie's faith increasingly pointed *toward* it.

After vigorously digging into the historical details, Strobel realized there was an avalanche of information pointing to Jesus's resurrection and, with it, his claim to being the unique Son of God. Lee realized, "It would require much more faith for me to maintain my atheism than to trust in Jesus of Nazareth."[3] So Lee trusted in Jesus, and years later he wrote *The Case for Christ*, detailing what he had discovered.

It would be six years after his coming to faith that Lee and I would meet on what would mark the beginning of our own ministry careers, as well as our three decades-plus of close friendship and ministry partnership. During that time I've had a front-row seat from which to see the amazing ways God uses his testimony and his *Story-Sharing* style to spiritually encourage, inform, and inspire many others to investigate and follow Christ themselves.

The Story-Sharing Contagious Faith Style

Those with the *Story-Sharing* style are skilled (or can become skilled) at articulating the details of their experiences with God and his grace. They illustrate in an experiential way the reality that life with God is better—even in hard times—and that anything given up to know and follow him is well worth the price.

They tend to be clear communicators, and they're adept at articulating the details of their experiences. So, when they describe to their coworkers or classmates what they did during the weekend or the summer break, their friends are usually interested.

Are you a storyteller? Is it easy for you to talk about things that are happening in your life? And when you do, are your listeners typically dialed in to what you're saying? Also, are you able to gauge their level of interest so you know how much detail to give and when to summarize your experiences or to draw your story to a close? If so, you would probably be good at this *Story-Sharing* approach.

Now, you may be a natural at talking about everyday things

you've experienced, but you're not yet delving into discussions about spiritual topics. That's okay; we're trying to get a sense of which approach would likely fit you and then take steps to develop and deploy it. So if you find yourself easily describing your trip to the lake or the exciting ballgame you went to with the family, it's likely that you could adapt your approach to highlight the spiritual activity of God in your life as well.

All of us who are followers of Jesus have a story to tell about his activity in our lives. In fact, Revelation 12:11 says that one of our primary weapons for winning spiritual battles is *the word of our testimony*. That's because the details of your journey from a self-centered life to one of serving Christ are a constant reminder that God is moving in you. Your story reinforces your own faith— and it's a powerful tool for sharing that faith with friends. As a result, it's important for each of us to think through the elements of our spiritual journey and how we might best describe them to others.

Our Experiential Culture

Something that's exciting about the *Story-Sharing* approach is that we live in a culture that increasingly values experience. As a result, many people today are not asking whether something is *true*, but whether it *works*. When applied to spiritual matters, many of our friends are not so concerned with the logic or evidence related to our beliefs, but whether or not those beliefs make a meaningful difference in our lives.

This emphasis can obviously have its downsides—and we'll talk about the importance of knowing and presenting God's truth in the next couple of chapters. But when people ask if Jesus has a significant influence in the life of his followers, we have a great answer, fleshed out by our account of what he has done, and continues to do, for us.

I love how John illustrates the importance of his experience with Jesus in the opening of his first letter. He describes what he and the other eyewitnesses had experienced: "That which was from the beginning, which we have *heard*, which we have *seen with our eyes*, which we have *looked at and our hands have touched*—this we proclaim concerning the Word of life. The life appeared; *we have seen it* and testify to it, and we proclaim to you the eternal life, which was with the Father and has *appeared to us*. We proclaim to you what we have *seen and heard*, so that you also may have fellowship with us. And our fellowship is with the Father and with his Son, Jesus Christ" (1 John 1:1–3, emphases mine).

While John's encounters with Jesus were direct and in-person, he nonetheless exemplifies how we can speak to others out of our own interactions with Jesus—drawing from what we've seen and heard of him in less direct ways. Our experiences with God can then inspire our friends, in turn, to seek out similar experiences with him—especially that of receiving his salvation and leadership in their own lives.

The Blind Man's Story

One of the best biblical examples of the *Story-Sharing Contagious Faith Style* being put into action is found in John 9. A man who had been born blind was sitting by the path where Jesus was walking. People in that culture assumed that blindness was due to some kind of sin—either in his life or the life of his parents.

So, this man had to live not only with his physical limitations but also with the spiritual stigma that went along with them. And it had been that way as long as he could remember.

But when Jesus saw him, he explained to his disciples that the man's condition was not due to any particular sin in anyone's life. Rather, he explained, "this happened so that the works of God might be displayed in him" (John 9:3).

This is remarkable! Jesus was saying that this guy was ordained by God to be in this situation so Jesus could show his miracle-working and life-changing power through him. I believe this included not just the restoration of his sight, but also the testimony this man would be to his fellow countrymen—especially to the religious leaders who were sure to take notice. And, in a similar way, I believe God designed you and me to be used in certain ways—including through our particular *Contagious Faith Styles*.

Jesus approached the man, "spit on the ground, made some mud with the saliva, and put it on the man's eyes. 'Go,' he told him, 'wash in the Pool of Siloam'" (John 9:6–7). The man followed Jesus's instructions, and within moments he was able to *see!*

But he barely had a chance to blink before he found himself on trial in front of the religious leaders. These were men who should have been excited to see the wonder-working power of God manifested in his life, but sadly that wasn't the case— particularly because the healing happened on the Sabbath. They were convinced Jesus had disobeyed God's laws, since he had broken their highly revered Sabbath rules.

"Give glory to God by telling the truth," they demanded of the formerly blind man. "We know this man is a sinner."

He replied, "Whether he is a sinner or not, I don't know. One thing I do know. I was blind but now I see!" (verses 24–25).

I love how focused he was in proclaiming God's work in his life. He refused to be drawn into their theological thickets. He stuck to his story. In effect, he said to them, "Look, fellas, I'm not going to debate you about the peripheral details. What I know is this: *I used to be blind, now I can see—deal with it!*"

What were they going to do—argue with his experience? Everyone knew this guy had been born blind; they couldn't deny that Jesus had given him his sight. Now the Pharisees wanted to quibble about the particular day on which it occurred, and why it's not permissible according to their rules for Jesus to heal people on the Sabbath. Talk about hard hearts!

Then, after the man patiently explained what Jesus had done for him (and them not liking it), they had the audacity to tell him to start again from the top of the story.

His response? "I have told you already and you did not listen," he replied in verse 27. "Why do you want to hear it again? Do you want to become his disciples too?"

That last question didn't go over very well with these self-righteous zealots, as you can imagine. They hurled insults at the man, saying emphatically that *he* was Jesus's disciple, not them. Instead, they claimed to follow Moses.

"But as for this fellow," they added in reference to Jesus, "we don't even know where he comes from" (verse 29).

Undaunted, the man shot back, "Now that is remarkable! You don't know where he comes from, yet he opened my eyes. We know that God does not listen to sinners. He listens to the godly person who does his will. Nobody has ever heard of opening the eyes of a man born blind. If this man were not from God, he could do nothing" (verses 30–33).

That was the *Story-Sharing* style mixed with a healthy dose of holy boldness! He used his spiritual experience as a spring-board into telling people about the Savior, whom he himself had just met moments earlier.

Jesus's Story-Sharing

In each of the *Contagious Faith Styles*, I've shown places where Jesus used the specific style being discussed. That's more challenging to do on this one, since Jesus could not say, as we can, "I once was lost, but now I'm found."

But Jesus did speak out of his experience in ways that modeled at least aspects of this approach. He said to his religious critics, for example, "You are from below; I am from above. You are of this world; I am not of this world" (John 8:23).

In other words, the people he was speaking to were, like us, ordinary human beings. Mere earthlings. But Jesus is not like us. He comes "from above." As the apostle John explains in John 3:16, "God so loved the world that he gave his one and only Son . . ." John also writes earlier in his Gospel, "The Word became flesh and made his dwelling among us. We have seen his glory, the glory of the one and only Son, who came from the Father, full of grace and truth" (John 1:14).

And Paul elaborates in Philippians 2:6–7, saying that even though Jesus was "in very nature God . . . he made himself nothing by taking the very nature of a servant, being made in human likeness"—all so he could come and pave the way for our salvation by dying on the cross for us.

And near the end of his earthly ministry, Jesus explained to his disciples: "I will be with you only a little longer. You will look for me . . . [but] where I am going, you cannot follow now, but you will follow later" (John 13:33, 36).

This was Jesus's own journey, and he often shared aspects of it for our benefit. It was *his* story that ultimately enabled us to have *our* stories of spiritual redemption—testimonies we can in turn share with others.

KEY SKILLS FOR EVERY CHRISTIAN

Whether or not the *Story-Sharing* style is your main approach, there are three *Key Skills* that are helpful for all of us as we engage people around the subject of our spiritual experience. These can help us better understand the person we're talking to and assist us in communicating our stories in ways that really connect with them.

1. Use Questions to Draw Out Your Friend's Spiritual Beliefs

We said earlier that the central focus of our story needs to be on how it will relate to the person with whom we're sharing it. But the only way we can effectively tailor our communications to that person is by first getting to know *their* story. And the way we can best get at that is by asking them open-ended questions and then really listening to what they tell us.

Jesus, as always, was the master. In fact, he often answered people's questions by asking his own. In this way he would draw people out, get to know their real thoughts and motivations, and make them all the more eager to see what he would say in reply. As Karen Lee-Thorp explains in her book, *How to Ask Great Questions*, "Jesus's questions were simple, clear, never condescending, always provocative. They made people think for themselves and examine their hearts. Jesus's questions were always fresh and attuned to the unique needs of the people he was talking to."[4]

Garry Poole adds in his groundbreaking book, *Seeker Small Groups*, "Questions are great conversation starters. They force people to think, look within themselves, examine their hearts, and search for answers. Just as questions were a great teaching tool for Jesus, questions are also an excellent tool in the hands of his followers. By simply raising a few good questions with your seeking friends, you can spark in-depth spiritual conversations. 'What is your religious background?' 'How have your beliefs changed over the years?' 'Where would you say you are now in your spiritual journey?'"[5]

More specific to the *Story-Sharing* approach, Poole adds that we need to "ask our neighbors about their stories, and then listen, really listen. Ask follow-up questions. And then listen some more. Non-Christians are eager to tell their stories, once they find a Christian willing to stop talking long enough to listen. Understand where they're coming from first. Only then will we earn the right to share our stories . . . and God's."[6]

I agree. And I'd add that by asking others about their backgrounds and encouraging them to talk first, you'll find any pressure you might be feeling start to subside as you relax and engage with them on the details of their lives. Then when you finally share your own story you'll be much more at ease, and they'll likely be more eager to listen.

2. Communicate Your Story around a Natural Outline

When it comes time to tell your story, it's helpful to have thought it through previously and organized it in a simple outline format—one that helps it flow naturally but which also gives you the flexibility to address things your friend shared about their experience. Putting it a different way, you should avoid the extremes of either inventing your outline on the spot, in which case it could get disjointed and confusing, or of presenting a memorized speech, which probably would come off as canned and impersonal.

Here is my suggested three-part outline:[7]

Discovery: What did you *discover* that helped shape your spiritual journey? What helped you reach the conclusion that you needed Christ and the salvation he offers? Was it when you were a child? Was it a process (it usually is)—or maybe a series of discoveries? Who or what were the main influences on your thinking? Were you immediately open, or was it a more gradual journey? This point might flow out of a dramatic experience you had all in one day, or it could be the summary of what you discovered over a longer season.

Decision: What did you *decide* based on that discovery?

This might have been a series of mini-decisions—for example, to search more deeply, to attend a discussion group or church service, or to talk to someone about your spiritual questions. But be sure to include an explanation of the *ultimate* decision you made to ask God for his forgiveness and leadership in your life, based on Jesus's payment on the cross for your sins. Also, try to explain what you did in transferable terms that your friend can understand and imitate. You can do this by being specific about what you understood, decided, and prayed.

Difference: What *difference* did that decision make in your life? One of the most important aspects of our testimony (especially to a friend who's trying to decide whether it's worth it to follow Christ) is the difference Jesus has made in your life. What have been the benefits? We need to be careful here not to describe the Christian life in flowery or overstated terms or to promise something the Bible does not guarantee: a life of unending success and happiness. But, yes, following Jesus is *better*. Jesus said he would give rest to the weary, and in John 10:10 he explained that he came so we "may have life, and have it to the full." He also said that "whoever loses their life for [his] sake will find it" (Matthew 10:39). Try to paint a positive but realistic picture, based on your own experience, of why it's better to follow Christ.

This simple framework is easy to remember and natural to follow. It's also very flexible. You can sum it up briefly or, if you have enough time and the other person shows genuine interest, you can expand upon it and go into much greater detail—but still follow this general flow. To illustrate how this can work, let's look back at a couple of the stories I've cited in this chapter.

Lee Strobel *discovered* that, in spite of his skepticism and initial disbelief, the evidence for Christianity is strong—that Jesus really did rise from the dead and therefore was, as he claimed to be, the divine Son of God. Based on that, Lee *decided* to put his trust in Jesus and to follow and serve him as best he knew how. And that has made a revolutionary *difference* in Lee's beliefs, priorities, and relationships.

The man in John 9 *discovered* that, in spite of being blind since birth, a miracle-worker who many believed to be the Messiah was walking near him, and that man, Jesus, was not only willing to talk to him but said he would heal him as well. Based on that, the blind man *decided* to trust Jesus and his power to do this miracle, and to demonstrate that trust by doing what Jesus told him to do—washing his eyes in the pool of Siloam (verses 6–7). And that made the *difference* that he was suddenly able to see! (verse 7).

This man's story also has another layer. The first was about his physical healing; the second is about his spiritual rebirth (verses 35–39). Here we see him later, after being interrogated by the religious leaders, talking with Jesus. It's actually then that he *discovers* that Jesus is the divine "Son of Man" (verse 35), so he *decides* to believe in him, and the *difference* it makes is that he immediately begins to worship Jesus (verse 38).

Here's one more example we haven't looked at yet, but it's the classic account of the apostle Paul sharing his story in Acts 26 in front of King Agrippa. Paul sums up his testimony by explaining that he had been a strict and loyal Pharisee who was convinced he needed to serve God by opposing the new movement of Jesus-followers.

But then, on his way to Damascus to persecute the believers there, he *discovered* that the crucified Jesus was alive—because Jesus appeared and spoke directly to him. In the midst of that miraculous appearance (and simultaneous blindness), Paul *decided* that he should stop resisting the risen Savior and begin to serve him instead. The *difference* that made was immediate and dramatic. Instead of persecuting followers of Jesus he became one himself, and he soon began leading more and more people to faith in Christ.

See how naturally this approach to *Story-Sharing* flows? So, what's your story, using this same three-part sequence? What did you *discover*? What did that lead you to *decide*? And what *difference* has that made in your life? I'd urge you to take a few minutes and write down your answers to those three questions right now, and then look for opportunities to practice telling others your story by following this flexible format.

Even more, I hope you'll consider gathering with a few friends from your church or fellowship and going through the six-week *Contagious Faith* video training course, where together you'll be able to develop and hone this approach further.[8]

3. Relate Your Story to Your Friend's Situation

There's one more *Key Skill* to discuss briefly. As much as possible, we need to connect our story to the life situation and concerns of the people we're talking to—and, ideally, we should do this at both the beginning and at the end of what we share.

Lee Strobel often does this by explaining, at the beginning, that his journey through skepticism is relevant to anyone who has spiritual doubts or questions—whether they're a believer or someone just considering the Christian faith. "You might not be an atheist like I was," he'll say. "But you probably wrestle with some of the same doubts and questions that I did at that time. Maybe the details of my journey will help you come to terms with some of the issues that trouble you."

Then, after he shares his story, including much of the evidence that convinced him Jesus is who he claimed to be, he'll put the ball back in the other person's court. He'll ask them, "In light of the information I learned and how it changed my life, what do you think your next steps might be?" Given the compelling nature of Lee's story and the information he learned, people often acknowledge that they need to trust Christ in the way he did.

I also like the way that Paul, in the example we saw in Acts 26, deliberately connected his experience to those of the people listening to him. He did this at the beginning, in verses 2–3. "King Agrippa," Paul begins, "I consider myself fortunate to stand before you today as I make my defense against all the accusations of the Jews, and especially so because you are well acquainted with all the Jewish customs and controversies. Therefore, I beg you to listen to me patiently." See how effectively he builds a conceptual bridge to the king by highlighting their areas of shared experience?

It's a winsome and powerful beginning that you can emulate, for example, by saying something like, "I'm really glad we're talking about this, Randall, because your studies in science seem to be leading you to very similar conclusions I reached when I first started at the university." Or, "What you shared about your challenging experiences with church when you were younger, Sarah, reminds me so much of what I went through. In fact . . ." and then you can talk about how these similar experiences affected you and how you were able to work through them, eventually trusting in Christ and letting him heal your past and guide your life.

Going back to Paul in Acts 26, you'll see how he again connected the elements of his testimony to his listeners after he had presented his story. In verses 25–27, after being challenged by a man named Festus, he applied his message to King Agrippa by boldly declaring to Festus, "What I am saying is true and reasonable. The king is familiar with these things, and I can speak freely to him. I am convinced that none of this has escaped his notice, because it was not done in a corner. King Agrippa, do you believe the prophets? I know you do."

This was a very effective way of projecting what he had shared onto the life of his high-profile listener—and if you read the entire story, you'll see that the king clearly got the point.

So let's follow these examples and, as much as possible, tether our story to the concerns and experiences of the people we're talking to, in an effort to show them once again that what we've found in Christ can help them in similar ways.

Cautions Concerning the *Story-Sharing* Style

Several important cautions are in order, related to this style.

Embrace Your Story

Don't underestimate the value of your testimony because it doesn't seem to be dramatic or exciting enough. The examples I gave earlier of an atheist finding faith and a blind man being given sight are thrilling, but they're not typical. More often our stories are more ordinary—as is mine.

I was a semi-religious kid raised in a churchgoing family. But I wrestled for a long time with how to apply my spiritual beliefs to my everyday life. For several years, especially during high school, I resisted the influence of God and the church in my life altogether. I wanted to have fun and adventure, and I didn't want anything or anyone getting in the way of that. But finally, as I was approaching my nineteenth birthday, I started to see through the thin veneer of the "fun" I was trying to have.

I was beginning to get glimpses into the truth of the verse that warns, "There is a way that appears to be right, but in the end it leads to death" (Proverbs 14:12). As my eyes were opening to the darkness in my own life, the brightness of Christ's life became increasingly attractive to me.

Finally, after years of struggle, on November 8, 1976, I gave up on going my own way. I yielded my life to Christ and asked him to not only forgive my many sins, but to lead me from that day forward. And you know what? *He has!* Ironically, my life suddenly became much more exciting. I realized that God had better adventures for me than I'd ever imagined for myself—ones that would stretch and grow me, while spiritually impacting the lives of others. This led, eventually, to me traveling and speaking all over the world, and it opened doors for me to write books to help people better understand and serve God.

My point? The story of a life turned from sin to the Savior is always significant, but it's not necessarily enthralling. They make movies about former atheists, gang members, and jihadists, but nobody is making a movie about *my* life. And that's okay. Those more dramatic stories relate well to certain groups of people, but mine—and maybe yours—resonates with those who have a formal religious background but who haven't really opened themselves up to the forgiveness and leadership of Christ.

Every testimony has an important role in building God's kingdom. Every changed life is a miracle. It's important for each of us to think through how we can effectively organize and articulate our stories and then share them until it feels natural. And for some Christians, perhaps including you, this will be their primary approach to sharing the Good News with others.

Be Honest

A second caution is to be honest and realistic about the details of your life. You probably weren't the worst person on the planet before you found God, and your life certainly isn't perfect now. Resist the temptation to overstate either side of that equation. Be honest about your personal ups and downs—both then and now. Also, ask the Holy Spirit, as well as mature believers in your life, for wisdom about which details of your experience are worth mentioning versus ones it would be better to skip. And make sure whatever is shared will ultimately point people back to Christ, and that it will honor him and his work in you.

Tailor to Your Audience

Something else to keep in mind is that even though this is your story, the point of it is to help the person you're sharing it with; it's to use your experience to assist them in understanding how God could work in *their* life. Let that priority be a guiding principle in deciding what to talk about, how much to say, and what to emphasize. Your story is multifaceted, and parts of it will connect better with some people than with others. The goal of sharing at least sections of it is to encourage whoever you're talking with to move forward with Christ in ways that reflect your experience with him.

Speak in Plain English

Don't try to impress people with lofty theological terminology. And maybe even more important: avoid religious clichés and church jargon. At best, you'll sound like you're from a different world. At worst, you'll be completely misunderstood. In Colossians 4:5–6 Paul warns us to act with wisdom toward outsiders, and to let our "conversation be always full of grace, seasoned with salt, so that you may know how to answer everyone."

So be gracious in how you communicate—but in addition to that, talk normally. This, by the way, is something we all struggle with at times. Something practical we can do to improve in this area is to invite Christian friends to tell us when we're talking in unclear or ineffective ways—and be ready to do the same for them. As Solomon said, "Iron sharpens iron" (Proverbs 27:17), so with each other's help we can all get better at expressing ourselves in ways that are understandable and effective.

The Extraordinary Impact of *Story-Sharing*

Robert was known for living on the edge, taking insane risks, and repeatedly dodging death. His success made him wealthy, but he gambled much of his money away. He once went to jail after trying to settle a dispute by using a baseball bat.

At the peak of his success he owned two private jets, which cost a fortune to fly—but he once ordered both of them into the air at the same time. Why? So he could sip champagne in one of them while looking at his name painted on the side of the other one!

Robert had no interest in God and often ridiculed Christians for their faith. Meanwhile, he lived a lifestyle of habitually breaking many of the Bible's commandments—and this continued until he was sixty-five years old.

Then one day he was out walking when he suddenly sensed God speaking to him. *Robert, I've rescued you more times than you'll ever know*, the inaudible voice said. *Now I want you to come to me through my Son Jesus.*

He was astounded. Why would God talk to him? And what was he supposed to do about it? Robert called one of the few Christians he knew and asked for advice. That friend urged him to read Lee Strobel's book *The Case for Christ*, which he did. The Holy Spirit used Lee's story, along with the evidence that had persuaded Lee to move from atheism to faith.

"All of a sudden I just believed in Jesus Christ. I did! I believed in him!" Robert later recounted. "I just got on my knees and prayed that God would put his arms around me and never, ever, ever let me go."

Robert's life changed radically. Soon, he was sharing his faith with whoever would listen. But he wanted the whole world to know, so he reached out to the pastor of a large church and asked him to baptize him on his televised broadcast, and to let him share his story briefly. When this happened, Robert shared his story with such simplicity and clarity that God moved powerfully throughout the sanctuary—and when the pastor asked if anyone else wanted to put their trust in Christ and be baptized in the same way, many began responding to the opportunity.

With "Amazing Grace" playing in the background, person after person—many with tears streaming down their cheeks—came to the front of the church to put their trust in Jesus. God moved in a powerful way that day, and by the time it was over, *700 people* had committed their lives to Christ!

Robert later became friends with Strobel after calling to thank him for writing his book. His biggest regret, he told him, was that he hadn't given his life to Jesus earlier. He challenged him, saying, "Lee, you have to tell people, 'Don't put this off! *Don't* put it off!'"

"There's just so much I want to do for God," he said again and again.

But time was running out for Robert. He was suffering from a lung condition that took his life just a few months later. When they held his funeral at his hometown in Montana, thousands showed up for it.

"Why would so many people want to honor a guy like Robert?" Strobel later wrote.

That's a natural question to ask, but only because I haven't told you the rest of the story. You see, nobody called Robert by his real name; they always referred to him instead by his nickname, which was *Evel*.

This unlikely Christian, known by the name *Evel Knievel*, risked his life to jump motorcycles over increasingly challenging obstacles, in the process landing in the *Guinness World Records* book for breaking more bones than any other human being.[9] Unexpectedly, extraordinarily, this once self-absorbed celebrity had been humbled and awed by God's undeserved love.

So while thousands of admirers flocked to his memorial service to pay tribute to Evel, his tribute went somewhere else. Before he died, Evel had asked for these words to be etched on his tombstone for all the world to see: *Believe in Jesus Christ*.[10]

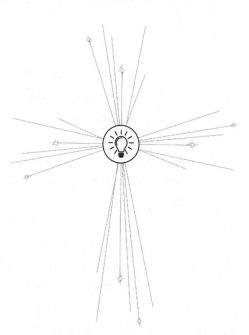

CHAPTER 6

STYLE #4:
REASON-GIVING

*But in your hearts revere Christ as Lord. Always
be prepared to give an answer to everyone who
asks you to give the reason for the hope that you
have. But do this with gentleness and respect.*

—1 PETER 3:15

"Here's what you need to understand," my Jehovah's Witness
friend insisted. "When the Bible says in John 1:3 that 'Through
him all things were made; without him nothing was made that
has been made,' it's not saying that Jesus is himself the Creator
God. Rather, it's simply telling us that after God first created
Jesus, then *everything else* was made through him."

It was a classic Watch Tower Society argument from a sincere man who had knocked on our door just moments earlier. He
and his companion were adamant in explaining that Jesus is not
Jehovah God, but a lesser created being who partnered with God

in making everything else. The implication, of course, is that the doctrine of the Trinity is false, and that in order to understand what the Bible really teaches I would need to join their group and start attending their services at the local Kingdom Hall.

"I understand that this is what you've been taught," I responded. "But you need to know there are serious problems with that position. First, that's not what the verse says. John 1:3 makes it clear that through Jesus, '*all* things were made'—so Jesus was not himself made, because he can't logically be part of that 'all.' And the verse goes on to underscore that fact by adding 'without him *nothing* was made that has been made.' And this squares with what we read about his identity a few minutes ago in John 1:1, where it says that Jesus ["the Word"—see verse 14] was *with* God (he was with the Father from eternity past), and that he *was* God (he is himself divine).

"Second, other passages in the New Testament tell us clearly that Jesus created all things. Colossians 1:16 says, for example, 'in him all things were created: things in heaven and on earth, visible and invisible, whether thrones or powers or rulers or authorities; all things have been created through him and for him.'

"And third, you need to account for the Old Testament passage of Isaiah 44:24, where it plainly tells us, 'This is what the LORD says—your Redeemer, who formed you in the womb: I am the LORD, the Maker of all things, who stretches out the heavens, who spreads out the earth *by myself*.' So who is the Creator? It's the Lord, our Redeemer, the true God—and he *alone* made everything! He didn't have any angels or other created beings there to help him, because he was 'the Maker of all things,' and he did it *by himself*!

"Putting this all together, this means that Jesus, along

with the Father and the Holy Spirit, is our one true Creator, Jehovah God."

I could tell that my new friend had not seen the Isaiah passage before and didn't know how to respond to its powerful message—though he certainly tried to challenge its clear implications. I held firm, and prayed silently that God would open his eyes, and those of his associate, to see what the Bible really teaches about the nature of God and the true identity of Jesus.

My Journey with the *Reason-Giving* Style

How did I get started with this *Reason-Giving* approach? Almost immediately after putting my trust in Jesus, I started sharing him with the people around me. Sometimes they would push back on what I was saying. "How do you know that's true?" they'd ask. "Maybe you just think that because it's what your parents believe," they'd add. "And besides, isn't it judgmental for you to think you're right and other people are wrong?"

I could tell many stories about interesting people and ideologies I encountered during that time. It was as if God were orchestrating a whole series of sincere religious people from a variety of worldview backgrounds, including not only the Jehovah's Witnesses but also the Latter Day Saints (Mormons), Muslims, members of The Way International, folks with Wiccan beliefs, as well as agnostics and atheists. Also, around this same time I took my first philosophy class at the local university, where our liberal professor questioned the allegedly simplistic beliefs of Christian students like me who believed in the reliability of the Bible and what he referred to as the traditional view of God.

All of this stretched me—but as I studied to answer these

challenges it served to build up my faith and help me become increasingly able to "demolish arguments and every pretension that sets itself up against the knowledge of God," and to "take captive every thought to make it obedient to Christ" (2 Corinthians 10:5).

If you'll rise to the challenge when people ask you hard questions about your beliefs, it can do the same for you. Studying to answer their objections will deepen your understanding and firm up your spiritual confidence. And you might just discover—as I did around the time I served in London several years later—that you, too, have the *Reason-Giving* style of sharing your faith.

The Reason-Giving Contagious Faith Style

"But in your hearts revere Christ as Lord," wrote Peter in his first epistle. He continued, "Always be prepared to give an answer to everyone who asks you to give the reason for the hope that you have" (1 Peter 3:15). This command is for all followers of Christ, but for some of us who have the *Reason-Giving Contagious Faith Style*, this is our main way of reaching out to others.

How about you? Are you unsatisfied with merely knowing what you believe, but also adamant about knowing *why* you believe it—why it makes sense? Are you logical, analytical, and inquisitive? Do you find yourself constantly checking things out—researching ideas to make sure you're correct in your understanding?

Some of us just have to *know!* And when we interact with others, we're generally more concerned about what they think and why they think it, than about how they feel about things. We resonate with the saying, "Facts don't care about our feelings."

More than that, we like to debate ideas. Once we're convinced that we have good reasons to believe what we believe, we naturally want to help others see things the way we do.

Can you relate to the *Reason-Giving* approach? Is this a style that might be natural for you? Right now you might just be sparring with people about general topics, whether related to business, current events, politics, or even everyday matters (for instance, which sports team or athlete is the best)—and why you're confident that's the case. But if you would focus on researching and discussing *spiritual* matters, God could use you in significant ways to answer people's questions, remove their intellectual roadblocks, and help them move toward trust in Christ, as well as to reinforce the faith of those who already know him.

Reasons and Evidence in Our Skeptical Culture

There's never been a greater need for believers who will develop and use the *Reason-Giving* style of evangelism. Our culture is drifting further and further away from the true God and the Christian worldview. Many people simply don't believe what they used to believe. It wasn't that long ago, at least here in the West, when almost everyone had some kind of religious training— whether through Sunday school, catechism, parochial school, or vacation Bible school. If you told them they needed Christ, they would probably acknowledge that to be true but add that they weren't ready to follow him just yet. The barrier was usually with the will, not the intellect.

By contrast, a lot of people today want to know how we can be sure God even exists at all, and, if he does, that Jesus was his Son. Many are now convinced that Jesus was just a good moral teacher—one who was completely misunderstood. As someone once put it to me, "If Jesus knew that you guys were worshiping him today, he'd roll over in his grave!"

I responded by reminding him that Jesus isn't *in* his grave. I continued by offering reasons we can know that Jesus claimed to be the divine Son of God, that he welcomed worship even while still here on earth, and that his purpose was to redeem people like us and turn us into his followers, both now and for eternity.

Fifty or sixty years ago, we wouldn't have faced many of these questions. But the trend of secularization continues and is accelerating. As people experience growing levels of confusion about spiritual matters and raise increasing numbers of objections to the Christian faith, we'll need more and more of us to be prepared to use this *Reason-Giving* style of evangelism.[1]

The Apostle Paul: Giving Reasons for Our Faith

Paul is a powerful New Testament example of the *Reason-Giving* style of evangelism. We see him putting this approach into action on Athens's Mars Hill in Acts 17, where he was speaking to a group of philosophers. This was a very different audience than he was used to addressing, but the passage reveals what motivated him. It says Paul "was greatly distressed to see that the city was full of idols" (verse 16). His love for these spiritually confused people—as well as his passion for God's glory—drove him to reach out to as many of them as possible.

Paul began his discourse in a clever way. He referred to an altar and inscription he'd noticed in their midst: TO AN UNKNOWN GOD (verse 23). Building on that phrase, he said to them, in essence, "Let me tell you about the God you don't know—because he's the *real* one!"

Then Paul laid out, in summary fashion, the story of our redemption:

- "The God who made the world and everything in it is the Lord of heaven and earth"—he is the Creator of all things (verse 24).
- He "does not live in temples built by human hands. And he is not served by human hands, as if he needed anything"—he is transcendent and self-sufficient (verses 24–25).
- "He himself gives everyone life and breath and everything else"—he doesn't depend on us. Rather, we depend on him (verse 25).
- "From one man he made all the nations, that they should inhabit the whole earth; and he marked out their appointed times in history and the boundaries of their lands. God did this so that they would seek him and perhaps reach out for him and find him, though he is not far from any one of us"—he orchestrated things in a way that would encourage us to seek and know him (verses 26–27, echoing Jesus in Matthew 7:7–8).
- "'For in him we live and move and have our being.' As some of your own poets have said, 'We are his offspring'"—here Paul is quoting two of *their* philosophers (probably Cretan philosopher Epimenides and Cilician Stoic philosopher Aratus) to make the biblical point that we were all created by God, and were made uniquely in his image (verse 28).
- "Therefore since we are God's offspring, we should not think that the divine being is like gold or silver or

stone—an image made by human design and skill. In the past God overlooked such ignorance, but now he commands all people everywhere to repent"—since God made us, it makes no sense for us to make and worship idols. Rather, it's time to grow up spiritually, and to turn away from our disobedient ways and toward him (verses 29–30).

- "For he has set a day when he will judge the world with justice by the man he has appointed. He has given proof of this to everyone by raising him from the dead"—he makes it clear that God will hold us morally accountable and proved all of this was true when he resurrected Jesus (verse 31).

Paul could have said much more (and, in fact, he probably did say more than was recorded by Luke). But what he *did* say packed quite a punch. Paul wasn't just talking about religious philosophy and ideas, though that's what they had expected. No, he was giving them rationale and reasons to believe his message about Jesus, especially the facts surrounding his resurrection from the grave.

Their response? Some rejected it, but others were curious and wanted to know more. They continued to talk with Paul, and we're told that a number of them became believers, including "Dionysius, a member of the Areopagus, also a woman named Damaris, and a number of others" (verses 32–34).

Here's the point we need to catch: *What Paul did here fit Paul!* He was knowledgeable, he was factual, he was logical, and he was confident. He had training and education—having been taught by Gamaliel, a legendary Jewish teacher of his day. Paul loved to debate truth, and he did so in ways that helped clear the intellectual path to the gospel—and ultimately to faith in Christ.

Elsewhere, Paul used phrases like, "we try to persuade others"

(2 Corinthians 5:11), "we demolish arguments," and "we take captive every thought to make it obedient to Christ" (2 Corinthians 10:5). We're also told that "every Sabbath [Paul] reasoned in the synagogue, trying to persuade Jews and Greeks" (Acts 18:4), and that while he was in Ephesus, "Paul entered the synagogue and spoke boldly there for three months, arguing persuasively about the kingdom of God" (Acts 19:8).

And as we saw in a different context, when Paul stood on trial for his faith in Acts 26, he articulated a strong case for Christianity, concluding by challenging his listeners with what they'd heard—never backing down in the slightest.

> "What I am saying is true and reasonable. The king is familiar with these things, and I can speak freely to him. I am convinced that none of this has escaped his notice, because it was not done in a corner. King Agrippa, do you believe the prophets? I know you do."
>
> Then Agrippa said to Paul, "Do you think that in such a short time you can persuade me to be a Christian?"
>
> Paul replied, "Short time or long—I pray to God that not only you but all who are listening to me today may become what I am . . ." (verses 25–29)

Jesus: Don't Believe My Words? Check Out My Works!

It's surprising to some people that Jesus, too, often used the *Reason-Giving* approach to reach others. He told his critics, "Don't believe me unless I carry out my Father's work. But if I do his work, *believe in the evidence of the miraculous works I have done, even if you don't believe me.* Then you will know and understand that the Father is in me, and I am in the Father" (John 10:37–38 NLT, emphasis mine).

Jesus was saying that if his critics were unwilling to take him at his word, then they ought to consider his supernatural activities instead, including his divine insights and miraculous interventions, and be convinced by those. He even went so far as to declare that those who had seen his miracles firsthand, but refused to repent, would be held more accountable at the judgment (see Matthew 11:20–24).

In fact, Jesus gave this stern warning about Capernaum, a place close to his heart and which Matthew called Jesus's "own town" (Matthew 9:1). "And you, Capernaum, will you be lifted to the heavens? No, you will go down to Hades. For if the miracles that were performed in you had been performed in Sodom, it would have remained to this day. But I tell you that it will be more bearable for Sodom on the day of judgment than for you" (Matthew 11:23–24).

This fits with the principle Jesus taught in Luke 12:48: "From the one who has been entrusted with much, much more will be asked." And part of what Jesus entrusted to the people around him were words and miraculous works that gave compelling evidence that he really was who he claimed to be: the divine Son of God.

Many other examples could be given, but let's just look at Jesus's response to John the Baptist. John was languishing in prison, and in his isolation, he began to doubt some of what he had been confident of in his earlier days regarding Jesus. So, he sent some of his disciples to Jesus and had them ask him point blank, "Are you the one who is to come, or should we expect someone else?" (Matthew 11:3).

Upon hearing this question, Jesus replied, "Go back and report to John what you hear and see: The blind receive sight, the lame walk, those who have leprosy are cleansed, the deaf hear, the dead are raised, and the good news is proclaimed to the poor. Blessed is anyone who does not stumble on account of me" (verses 5–6).

Jesus didn't tell John's disciples to go and challenge John to "just have more faith," or to "pray and read his Bible more." No, he gave them *reasons* to reinforce John's faith. Specifically, he pointed to the miracles he had performed as evidence of his identity, and he showed that he was fulfilling ancient predictions about the Messiah, the one who "heals all your diseases" (Psalm 103:3) and who would "proclaim good news to the poor" (Luke 4:16–21, especially verse 18, fulfilling Isaiah 61:1–2).

Jesus employed the *Reason-Giving* approach by pointing to evidence related to his own supernatural activities and fulfilled prophecies. He did this to clear away the doubts and objections of his listeners and to pull them toward faith in him.

KEY SKILLS FOR EVERY CHRISTIAN

It is important for all of us as followers of Christ to be able to give reasons for our faith, whether or not the *Reason-Giving* approach is our main style. Let's explore three *Key Skills* related to this area.

1. Be Prepared to Give Sound Answers and Evidence

Many people are just a good answer or two away from being ready to put their trust in Christ. John Swift, for example, a commercial banker from Chicago, said to me, "I'd *like* to become a Christian, but I still have a few questions that are hanging me up." In particular, it didn't seem possible to him that a man like Jesus could die a violent death on a cross and then come back from the dead three days later.

"Everything I've ever seen supports the fact that dead people simply stay in the grave and their bodies rot there—or get eaten by wild dogs," John explained wryly. "Why should I believe it was any different for Jesus?"

It was a great question. Why put our faith in a claim that contradicts everything we've ever experienced? But something wasn't adding up. John had already acknowledged to me that there is a God, so I decided to draw out the implications of that belief.

"Let me ask you something, John," I began. "If there is a God who is powerful enough to create the entire universe out of nothing, do you really think it would be hard for him to raise Jesus from the dead three days after he was crucified?"

"Well . . . I've never really thought about that before," he said, as a light seemed to be turning on in his mind. "But I suppose that wouldn't be that big of a deal for a divine Creator, would it?"

"No, I don't think it would—in fact, as one of my former professors used to explain, to a God who can create a universe, things like virgin births and resurrections from the dead would be like child's play!"

While he was considering that, I asked him what alternative theories he thought could possibly make sense. "If Jesus didn't rise from the dead," I asked, "then what do you think happened to his body? The early reports tell us that the tomb was empty."

With that, we talked about how neither the Jewish leaders nor the Roman authorities had any motive to move or hide the body—quite the opposite. And the disciples were completely demoralized and hiding in fear for their lives. They had neither the motive nor the means to try to steal the body of their crucified friend. And not only was there the empty tomb, but also multiple eyewitnesses who had seen the risen Jesus, talked with him, touched him, and even eaten with him—and several of them wrote early accounts of what they had seen and heard.

We spent about an hour talking about the evidence for Jesus's resurrection. At the close of our conversation, I loaned him a book that would give him further information, and I challenged him to read the section on the resurrection and to consider becoming a Christian by Easter, which was only about a month away. "That way you'll be able to finally celebrate the holiday for its real meaning," I told him.

John took the challenge, read the book, did further research, and I was delighted to find out later that a few days before Easter he gave his life to Christ. Undoubtedly, God used a number of influences to bring John to faith, but he would tell you the evidence and information he learned related to the resurrection of Jesus were vital parts of that mix.

I hope you're seeing how important it is to "give an

answer to everyone who asks you to give the reason for the hope that you have." God can use *you* to help remove the intellectual roadblocks that keep people from trusting in Christ. But you'll need to get ready.

How? First, study your Bible regularly. Read it not only devotionally, but also in order to find answers to the issues that concern your friends. Make notes in the margins so you can better retain and find that information when you need it.

Do the same with other books that give evidence and answers related to our faith. There's no substitute for exposing yourself to great written materials. Try to read a book on Christian apologetics each month. Read broad overviews of the evidence and answers we have for our faith, and then delve into additional ones that address specific questions your friends are asking.

Also, you might want to consider doing what I've learned to do almost daily—listen to audiobooks on your smartphone. They're convenient to buy and download, and you'll have them with you all the time. Once you've trained yourself to do this, you can enjoy good books in your car while you drive, and you can listen on headphones if you fly on business trips, or even while you work out, clean the house, or mow the lawn. Turn this into a habit, and you'll be amazed at how many books you can get through each year.

I also find it helpful to watch videos on relevant topics online, and to listen to podcasts or radio programs on related matters. Once you find teachers and ministries you trust, there's an almost endless supply of free resources to expand your knowledge base. See the *Recommended Resources* section in the back of this book for ideas on some of the best books, websites, and ministries with this kind of information.

As you study these matters, keep in mind that there are two facets to our *Reason-Giving* task: *offense* and *defense*. The *offense* is the offering of positive evidence for Christianity. It's giving your friends reasons to consider the claims of Christ. The *defense* is giving good answers to the objections they raise related to your faith.

Here are a few of the most common objections people bring up concerning our faith, along with short responses distilled from my book, *The Questions Christians Hope No One Will Ask (With Answers):*[2]

- *"What makes you so sure that God exists at all—especially when you can't see, hear, or touch him?"*

   [Short answer: We believe in many things we can't see or feel—like love, hope, and justice. And oxygen! We can confidently believe in God based on our experience of him, as well as the evidence related to the beginning of the universe, the design in the creation—including the astonishing ways it is fine-tuned to support life—and the reality of objective moral standards by which human beings know right and wrong.]

- *"Why trust the Bible, a book based on myths and full of contradictions and mistakes?"*

   [Short answer: People who have a bias against the miraculous call accounts of God's activity *myths* because they rule out anything supernatural, often without even examining the evidence. Also, most of what they call contradictions in the Bible are really just differences in the perspectives and degree of details reported by the various eyewitnesses to the events. The Bible demonstrates remarkable accuracy and consistency, as well as divine insight into the human heart and condition.]

- *"Everyone knows that Jesus was a good man and a wise teacher—but why try to make him into the Son of God, too?"*

  [Short answer: This objection overlooks the historical evidence showing that Jesus fulfilled numerous Old Testament prophecies of the coming Messiah, that he did a variety of miracles in the presence of even hostile eyewitnesses, that he described himself in divine terms and willingly received worship, and that he proved it was all true by rising from the dead (see Acts 2:22–24).]

- *"How could a good God allow so much evil, pain, and suffering—or does he simply not care?"*

  [Short answer: This difficult question is best addressed by the Christian worldview. It explains that we live in a fallen world in which "you *will* have trouble" (John 16:33a, emphasis mine), where God allows us the freedom to obey or turn away from him (because real love always entails the ability *not* to love; see Joshua 24:15), where he promised to walk with us through every valley—"but take heart! I have overcome the world" (John 16:33b,

Matthew 28:20, and Psalm 23), where God's justice will finally prevail (see Revelation 20:11–15), where he promises us as his followers to bring good out of everything we experience (see Romans 8:28), and where he cared enough to come as a man and he "suffered once for sins, the righteous for the unrighteous, to bring you to God" (1 Peter 3:18).]

- *"Why should I think that heaven really exists—and that God sends people to hell?"*

   [Short answer: We have thousands of accounts of near-death experiences by people around the world that testify to the reality of the afterlife—often with details that are virtually impossible to explain any other way. But our best evidence is the testimony of Jesus, who came from heaven, and who assures us heaven is our ultimate home (see John 3:13; John 14:1–4). Also, God doesn't send anyone to hell. He sent his Son to die for our sins and open the gates of heaven to everyone (see John 3:16), but we must receive the offer of the gospel (see John 1:12) or pay the penalty for our own sins (see Romans 6:23). The choice—and the responsibility—is ours (see Revelation 22:17).]

These are challenging questions, to be sure. But they, and many others like them, are objections we don't have to be afraid of or shrink back from answering, because what we believe is true. No, the answers aren't simple or wrapped neatly in a bow—but they make sense and point to the trustworthiness of our Christian beliefs. And I'm convinced that the more deeply you study them the more confident of this you'll become, and that you'll begin to see them not as issues to avoid but as entrées into fruitful conversations about the truth of our faith.

2. Respond to Questions with Gentleness and Respect

The verse I've quoted several times, 1 Peter 3:15, has a short ending that we need to underscore. It is vitally important in our efforts to lead people toward Christ. It's a qualifier that tells us how to "give an answer to everyone"—specifically, it says we are to "do this with gentleness and respect."

No matter how impressive an answer we might present to someone, if they see us as rude or arrogant and unwilling to treat them with dignity, then they will likely reject the response we've given. *You might be right,* they're thinking—*but I don't want to be like you!*

But if we winsomely and lovingly listen to their questions and respond in a way that doesn't shame them or make them feel like we think we're smarter or better than they are, then they'll naturally become more open to our answers. *I feel valued and respected,* they'll begin thinking—*and your information makes sense. I'd like to be more like you!*

Of course, this kind of attitude also makes us more like Jesus. To a world of spiritually beleaguered people, he said in Matthew 11:28–29 (emphasis mine): "Come to me, all you who are weary and burdened, and I will give you rest. Take my yoke upon you and learn from me, *for I am gentle and humble in heart, and you will find rest for your souls.*" That kind of an approach is spiritually magnetic!

3. Move from Good Answers to the Good News

The renowned apologist Josh McDowell once said that we should give just enough information to answer a person's question, but then get back to the gospel. I couldn't agree more. Our goal, again, is not to win arguments; it's to win people.

"Go and make disciples," Jesus commanded in Matthew 28:19. That's our central purpose. Yes, presenting evidence for Christianity and answering objections are important elements in that process—but we need to get back consistently to the message of Christ.

"The gospel," Paul tells us in Romans 1:16, "is the power of God that brings salvation to everyone who believes." That's why I stress that *good answers should ultimately point people back to the Good News of the gospel.*

Cautions Concerning the *Reason-Giving* Style

Here's some advice for using the *Reason-Giving* approach.

Clarify the Question

Before giving somebody your *reasons*, make sure you really understand their *questions*. Ask them what they believe about spiritual matters, how they arrived at their conclusions, and whether that's what they've always believed. If not, what led them to change their thinking? Are they confident about what they believe now? Do they have reasons that support their opinions, or are they mostly holding onto things they grew up with? Ask, and then really listen. In doing this, you'll know better who you're talking to, and you'll earn the right to offer your thoughts as well.

Resist the temptation to move too quickly to *Reason-Giving*. Asking people good questions, even in response to some of *their* questions, is a wise way to deepen the conversation and win their respect. Jesus was the master questioner, and we can learn a lot from his approach.[3]

Study Up

Do your homework. Peter said to "be prepared" (1 Peter 3:15). It's not enough to have an inclination toward this approach—you must really study. That will take time and energy spent reading and researching, and it will need to be an ongoing effort. There's always more to learn and new objections to address.

Admit It When You Don't Know

Don't make up answers. When you don't know something (and that will often be the case, especially at the beginning), don't pretend you do. Instead, admit that you haven't read up on that area yet and, if needed, ask the person for more information.

One time I struck up a conversation with a young lady who was playing her guitar at the mall. As I started talking about my faith in Jesus, she politely informed me that, for her, Jesus was just one of many prophets. She explained that she was a Bahá'í—a member of a worldwide faith community that follows the prophet Bahá'u'lláh.

I had no idea what or who she was talking about. So, I asked her lots of questions—and I went home and researched the topic further. Then I got back to her to share what I had learned, what my concerns were, and why I thought she should consider the biblical gospel over and above what she'd been taught.

You can do the same. *Admit you don't know, ask questions, do research,* and *come back with good answers.* You'll demonstrate humility, engage the other person, show you care enough to study their beliefs, and provide genuinely helpful information. Plus you'll learn a lot along the way. Practice this approach consistently over time, and you will have a rapidly growing reservoir of reasons to draw from.

Win People, Not Arguments

Offer good arguments for your faith, but don't devolve into argumentativeness. As soon as you let emotions get in the way of respectful conversation, you've strayed from the goal. Our purpose is to win *people,* not points. Also, be careful in deciding which issues you're willing to discuss with unbelievers. Hint: that generally should not include trivial differences about obscure Bible verses, peripheral doctrinal issues, in-house denominational disputes, or mere curiosity questions. Debating these matters usually generates more heat than light, and it rarely does anything to move the person toward Christ.

Ask yourself, *Is this really worth discussing? Will it help lead my friend to the Savior—or is it an unnecessary detour?* Then, as much as possible, stick to central issues.

Paul's admonition to Timothy squares with this. "Don't have anything to do with foolish and stupid arguments, because you know they produce quarrels. And the Lord's servant must not be quarrelsome but must be kind to everyone, able to teach, not resentful. Opponents must be gently instructed, in the hope that God will grant them repentance leading them to a knowledge of the truth" (2 Timothy 2:23–25).

Expect a Little Tension

Don't back off from presenting the gospel because you're afraid the other person might not like what you say. This is one of our greatest challenges in the church today. A lot of Christians—especially younger ones—think it's unkind or even unloving to ever disagree with someone's ideas. They've convinced themselves that the highest value in a friendship is to consistently keep things peaceful and harmonious.

I understand the temptation to think that way, but Jesus said following him would sometimes bring division (see Luke 12:51–53). That's not the goal, of course, but the surpassing value of your friend coming to know God makes the possibility of relational ripples well worth the risk. In fact, offering your friend reasons to follow the One who offers salvation is the most loving thing you can do for him.

Speaking from experience, this can put temporary tension in a relationship. But as God works in your friend over time, that tension can get replaced by a spiritual bond that is stronger than anything you can imagine—one that will last for eternity. So, yes, giving reasons for your faith has risks, but the potential results make those risks well worth it.

 ## The Extraordinary Impact of Answers and Evidence

"A Skeptic's Surprise" was a *Reason-Giving* event that we designed to reach out to Jewish people in our community. It was an exciting night, and the speaker's story gave a compelling account of a highly reluctant seeker slowly finding faith in Jesus, his Messiah.

Don Hart, a Jewish businessman, hesitantly attended that event. Upon leaving, Don couldn't get the message out of his mind. Suddenly he was thinking about spiritual questions he'd never considered before. *Could the messianic prophecies in the Old Testament really point to Jesus of Nazareth? Did Jesus really provide evidence that he was the Messiah? Are there solid reasons to believe in Jesus's miracles—especially the resurrection? Could he become a follower of Jesus without losing his Jewish identity?*

Don tracked me down to discuss his concerns. When we met in my office at the church, I immediately sensed his sincerity. He listened intently as I answered his questions. He wrote out many of my responses and jotted down the names of the books I encouraged him to read. Then when we'd get together again, he would have one or two of those books with him, the pages dog-eared and highlighted—and he'd always show up with a fresh set of questions.

Incredibly, after months of meeting and discussing his seemingly endless flow of concerns, everything began to culminate when Don started talking about—*of all things*—attending seminary! At first, I thought he was joking, but then he asked if I would write a letter of recommendation to help him get into a top evangelical graduate school.

"I'd be happy to, Don," I responded, "except I think you've gotten things a bit out of order. Don't you suppose it would be a good idea to become a *Christian* first—*then* consider going to a Christian seminary?"

With a twinkle in his eye, Don admitted there was a certain

logic to what I was saying. This led into one more conversation about some of his remaining concerns. Finally, Don acknowledged that he had found satisfactory answers to most of his questions, and with great joy he prayed with me to receive Jesus as his Messiah and Savior.

Don has been living an exciting adventure ever since that day! Though already in his fifties at the time, he did enroll at the seminary, where he rapidly grew in his understanding of God and the Bible. A couple of years later he graduated, and since then he has served as a biblical counselor, encouraging others in *their* spiritual journeys. And occasionally Don even gets to pray with someone to trust in Jesus, just as I had been given the privilege of doing with him.

Whenever I think of Don, I marvel at the importance of giving people reasons to consider the claims of Christ.

So, let me ask you: Who's the person in your life who might be just one or two good answers away from trusting in Jesus as their Savior? Are you ready to respond to the issues that friend might raise? What's your next step toward engaging him or her in a conversation? Get ready and take that step—and watch to see what God might do through it!

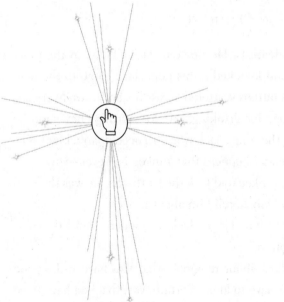

CHAPTER 7

STYLE #5:
TRUTH-TELLING

But how can they call on him to save them
unless they believe in him? And how can they
believe in him if they have never heard about
him? And how can they hear about him unless
someone tells them?

—ROMANS 10:14 NLT

"Uncle Jack" looked tough, talked tough, and *was* tough. He was a title-winning bodybuilder. He had been in and out of jail most of his life. One time, he choked the two policemen who tried to arrest him, rendering them both unconscious.

Jack was bad to the bone.

But he had one thing going for him: his friend Bob Daly desperately wanted him to know Christ. He felt hesitant to share the gospel with Jack himself, though—so he dared his friend Ralph "Yankee" Arnold to reach out to Jack instead.

Yankee was fearless. He drove to Jack's home in the inner city of Denver and knocked at his door. Jack came to the door with no shirt on, tattoos scattered across his body, two beer cans in his hands—one for drinking, one for spitting chew (and he tried not to mix them up). Jack was also accompanied by Lobo, the biggest German Shepherd that Yankee had ever seen.

Undaunted, Yankee told Jack the truth: that he was there on a dare from Bob Daly to tell him about Jesus.

"Well, I don't know Jesus," Jack responded. "But I do know Bob—so come on in."

Jack had heard about religion—that you have to be good enough; that you have to look a certain way; that you have to go to church if you want to make it to heaven. Jack could never do all of that. He told Yankee he knew he was going to hell, so he figured he might as well have fun before he got there.

Yankee sat across the kitchen table from Jack and shared the Good News with him. For the first time, Jack heard the message of grace—that there is a God who loves him so much he sent his Son to die for him. That Jesus paid the price Jack deserved to pay for his sins. And that it was through faith in Christ alone that he could be forgiven.

Jack had never been told *that* truth before. When Yankee asked him if what he said had made sense, Jack responded in the most emphatic way he knew how: "Hell, yeah!" And before their time together was over, he trusted in Jesus Christ, as did his wife Earlene, who had been listening as they talked.

The night Yankee boldly shared the true gospel message with Jack, Jack was transformed from the inside out. He immediately determined to tell everyone he knew about Christ. The next day, he went to his job at the meatpacking plant and led a coworker named Thumper to Christ. The day after that he went to Thumper's house and shared the gospel with Thumper's family, returning night after night until he'd explained the gospel as clearly as he could. Over the course of two weeks, this family came to faith.

One by one, Jack's friends and family members started trusting in Jesus. One person he'd shared the gospel with was Uncle Bob, who worked as a bouncer at a bar in Denver. One night when Bob found himself sitting in a squad car watching paramedics try to resuscitate a man he'd beaten in retaliation for stabbing his best friend, he remembered that message. Knowing the man's death would mean a lifetime in prison, he called out to God and said, "If you help them save that man, then I'll serve you the rest of my life and tell everyone I can about Jesus!"

By God's grace that man did recover, and with God's help, Bob followed through on his promise. A year later he attended Florida Bible College, where he later graduated—and he has been serving the Lord ever since then.

Over time, most of Jack's relatives came to Christ, including his nephew Greg Stier. Like his Uncle Jack and Uncle Bob, Greg also felt an immediate passion to share the Good News with others. He earned a degree at Colorado Christian University, and then went into pastoral ministry in Denver, not far from where he'd grown up.

A few years later, on April 20, 1999, two students at nearby Columbine High School opened fire on their classmates, killing twelve students and one teacher, while injuring twenty-one others. It was an event that shocked the world, and God used it to change the trajectory of Stier's life.[1]

He soon launched Dare 2 Share Ministries with the goal of

discipling and training high school students to share the gospel with their friends and family members. Since that time, Stier has helped train well over a million students to do just that in direct and compelling ways.[2]

This story illustrates the power of the *Truth-Telling Contagious Faith Style*, which was effectively modeled by Yankee, then by Uncle Jack and Uncle Bob, and now by Greg Stier and many of the students he has trained all over the country.

It may be your style as well!

The Truth-Telling Contagious Faith Style

Truth-Telling types are bold, confident, and direct. They're effective at getting to the point and bringing truth to bear in a variety of situations. They tend to have hard-hitting personalities, and they're often action-oriented leaders. They don't like a lot of small talk, and they don't beat around the bush. They zero in on what's important, and they generally do so quickly.

Perhaps that sounds like you. You may not actually be sharing your faith yet, but if you have this kind of approach then you can see how your assertiveness already plays out in your family, in interactions with friends, and with people at work. You like to get to the bottom of things, to figure out problems and set a course of action, and to make a difference. You probably focus more on accomplishing the goal at hand than the immediate feelings of the people you're interacting with. You're a change agent.

Now, if you'd apply your direct approach to presenting your faith to others, then you could become a powerful influence in leading people to Jesus. Compared to the other four *Contagious Faith Styles*, you'll probably find it relatively easy to raise spiritual topics of conversation, to get to the point of discussing the actual gospel message, and to challenge people to take action on the truth you've presented. You can be used by God to awaken them from their spiritual slumber and help them get off the fence to follow Christ.

We certainly need more of the *Truth-Telling* style in our culture today. Scripture warned us long ago about what people would be like in the future—and its description sounds a lot like what we're seeing today: "People will be lovers of themselves, lovers of money, boastful, proud, abusive, disobedient to their parents, ungrateful, unholy, without love, unforgiving, slanderous, without self-control, brutal, not lovers of the good, treacherous, rash, conceited, lovers of pleasure rather than lovers of God—having a form of godliness but denying its power" (2 Timothy 3:2–5).

This describes many who are outside the church, but also some who are *inside* as well—whose hearts and lives remain unchanged. People like this will often be difficult to reach through the other approaches we've discussed. But a direct biblical challenge from a godly *Truth-Telling* Christian will often shake them up and help them see the destructive path they're traveling. This, along with the convicting influence of the Holy Spirit, can help many of them turn around to trust and obey the Savior.

Peter: Truth-Teller for Christ

A great New Testament example of the *Truth-Telling* style is the apostle Peter who, filled with the Holy Spirit, stood up on the Day of Pentecost in Jerusalem—the city where Jesus had been crucified just a few weeks earlier—and proclaimed the unadulterated truth of the gospel to a mostly Jewish audience (Acts 2).

Prior to speaking, though, Peter and his fellow Jesus-followers generated curiosity among these thousands of "God-fearing Jews from every nation under heaven" (verse 5) who had gathered, by telling them the "wonders of God" in their own native tongues (verse 11). Recognizing this as something supernatural, the crowd asked for an explanation. Peter "raised his voice and addressed the crowd: 'Fellow Jews and all of you who live in Jerusalem, let me explain this to you; listen carefully to what I say . . .'" (verse 14).

In bold and direct terms, Peter declared: "Jesus of Nazareth was a man accredited by God to you by miracles, wonders and signs, which God did among you through him, as you yourselves know. This man was handed over to you by God's deliberate plan and foreknowledge; and you, with the help of wicked men, put him to death by nailing him to the cross. But God raised him from the dead, freeing him from the agony of death, because it was impossible for death to keep its hold on him" (verses 22–24).

Peter was just warming up! He went on to give them more details, deftly citing references to prophetic passages in the Old Testament that were being fulfilled in their midst. Then he summarized his message: "Therefore let all Israel be assured of this: God has made this Jesus, whom you crucified, both Lord and Messiah" (verse 36).

Clearly the Holy Spirit was at work, speaking through Peter's straightforward message and convicting hearts. Knowing what he had said was true, they asked urgently, "Brothers, what shall we do?" (verse 37).

Peter was prepared with an answer. He had already proclaimed that "everyone who calls on the name of the Lord will be saved" (verse 21). But now he explained what that looks like:

"Repent and be baptized, every one of you, in the name of Jesus Christ for the forgiveness of your sins. And you will receive the gift of the Holy Spirit. The promise is for you and your children and for all who are far off—for all whom the Lord our God will call" (verses 38–39).

God used Peter's *Truth-Telling* approach in an amazing way, with 3,000 people responding in faith and declaring their loyalty to Christ by being baptized that very day, becoming members of Jesus's newly formed church.

But here's what I want to underscore: *what Peter did in this situation authentically fit Peter!* God had given him a *Truth-Telling* personality. Peter was naturally bold, direct, and hard-hitting. He was also the first to speak up, right or wrong!

Thankfully, Peter was usually *right*. ("Blessed are you . . . for this was not revealed to you by flesh and blood, but by my Father in heaven," Jesus said to him in Matthew 16:17.) But occasionally Peter was spectacularly *wrong*. ("Get behind me, Satan! You are a stumbling block to me; you do not have in mind the concerns of God, but merely human concerns," Jesus said to him in Matthew 16:23, just six verses after the previous quote.)

Once fully trained and anointed with God's Spirit, though, Peter became an unstoppable force for sharing the gospel. And his God-given *Truth-Telling* style made him the ideal spokesman on the Day of Pentecost in Acts 2, and in many other settings.

Jesus, the Ultimate Truth-Teller

Jesus frequently employed this direct *Truth-Telling* approach as well. Think of his interactions with Nicodemus in John 3. Nicodemus came to talk to him at night, perhaps so he wouldn't be seen by others, since he was not only a Pharisee but also a member of the Jewish ruling council (verse 1).

Nicodemus began the conversation by affirming Jesus and his ministry: "Rabbi, we know that you are a teacher who has come from God. For no one could perform the signs you are doing if God were not with him" (verse 2). But rather than responding to this flattery, Jesus got to the point and told him what he needed to hear: "Very truly I tell you, no one can see the kingdom of God unless they are born again" (verse 3).

Don't miss the audacious nature of Jesus's response! Nicodemus was one of the top religious authorities in Israel, but Jesus skips conventional niceties and tells him directly that neither he nor anyone else is going to go to heaven unless they humble themselves and receive a spiritual birth from God.

To his credit, Nicodemus seems to avoid taking offense at Jesus's challenge, and instead asks clarifying questions. Jesus answers, making it clear that neither Nicodemus's great learning nor his religious performance—even as an elite Pharisee—would make him right with God. He still needed the spiritual birth that God alone could give him.

Based on the fact that after the crucifixion Nicodemus was there to help Joseph of Arimathea treat and wrap Jesus's body and place it in the tomb (see John 19:38–42), it seems pretty certain that Jesus's challenge to him yielded its intended result.

We can find many examples of Jesus's *Truth-Telling* approach, but here are just a few of his hard-hitting quotes—often spoken to challenge the religious authorities.

"Your mistake is that you don't know the Scriptures, and
you don't know the power of God" (Mark 12:24 NLT).

"You study the Scriptures diligently because you think
that in them you have eternal life. These are the very
Scriptures that testify about me, yet you refuse to
come to me to have life" (John 5:39–40).

"You are from below; I am from above. You are of this
world; I am not of this world. I told you that you would
die in your sins; if you do not believe that I am he, you
will indeed die in your sins" (John 8:23–24).

And perhaps the quintessential example was when Jesus
declared to all who were listening: "I am the way and
the truth and the life. No one comes to the Father
except through me" (John 14:6).

Why would Jesus make such bold and exclusive statements?
Well, first, because he knew they were true. And second, because
he understood—as all who have the *Truth-Telling Contagious Faith
Style* must learn—that "the truth will set you free" (John 8:32).

KEY SKILLS FOR EVERY CHRISTIAN

The *Truth-Telling* style may or may not be your main
approach but, as with the other evangelistic styles, there
are elements related to it that are vitally important for
every follower of Christ. Here are three *Key Skills* for all
of us to practice in our lives.

1. Be Bold in Initiating Spiritual Conversations

I sometimes hear discussions among Christians—including
on social media—about how we need to be careful to not

come on too strong with our faith. "There's nothing that more quickly shuts down someone's willingness to talk," the refrain goes, "than a pushy believer who's always forcing his or her beliefs on the people around them."

My response? "I completely agree—but you're describing only a very small fraction of the Christians out there. So maybe we should talk about the real problem, which is the large number of Christ-followers who virtually never talk about their faith at all!" It's much easier—and much more appealing—to criticize the overbearing believer who overdoes it with evangelism, than it is to admit that we tend toward fearfulness and overcautiousness ourselves. But that's almost always the greater issue.

"The Spirit God gave us does not make us timid, but gives us power, love and self-discipline," wrote Paul. "So do not be ashamed of the testimony about our Lord or of me his prisoner . . ." (2 Timothy 1:7–8).

Can you relate to this warning? Be honest!

Maybe it would help if I confessed that I often struggle with this myself—despite the fact that I write and speak about the topic. I'm often tempted to let opportunities go by. I don't want to be perceived as an obnoxious Christian who never lets up on the God-talk, and I avoid intruding on people's private world or becoming someone who tries to tell everyone else what they should believe or how they should live their lives. If you'll remember, I was the one who was reluctant to knock on doors in London to tell people about Jesus. Also, I was the one who was hesitant to talk to my friend Peggy about my faith.

Yes, more often than I'd like to admit I tend toward

timidity. So, I have to repeatedly declare war on this tendency and push back against it. I must rehearse, meditate upon, and pray over verses such as 2 Timothy 1:7–8, and ask God to take away my cautious streak, and to increase his power, love, and discipline in my life. And maybe you do too.

This is, of course, a prayer God loves to answer, since we're praying rock-solidly according to his will. Jesus said, "The harvest is plentiful, but the workers are few. Ask the Lord of the harvest, therefore, to send out workers into his harvest field. Go! I am sending you out like lambs among wolves" (Luke 10:2–3).

In other words, he's sending *you and me!*

It might also be helpful to remember something we talked about earlier: Your friends are more interested in spiritual matters than you think they are. You'll find out this is true when you start talking to more of them about it. So, take more risks and dive into more faith-related conversations, and you'll see that this is true.

Still not sure? You might be encouraged by reading Acts 4, where Peter and John were brought before the religious leaders and sternly told not to talk about Jesus anymore (verse 18). Their response? They threw caution to the wind and pointedly challenged their challengers: "Which is right in God's eyes: to listen to you, or to him? You be the judges! As for us, we cannot help speaking about what we have seen and heard" (verses 19–20).

Not only that, but upon their release, Peter and John went back and reported all that had happened to their fellow church members—and how did they respond? They prayed together, "Now, Lord, consider their threats and *enable your servants to speak your word with great boldness*" (verse 29, emphasis mine). And the result? "After they prayed, the place where they were meeting was shaken. And they were all filled with the Holy Spirit and spoke the word of God boldly" (verse 31).

They didn't ask God for more protection, relief from the growing persecution, or wisdom to find a way out of their spiritual predicament. They prayed for more *boldness!* We, the church, have a rich spiritual heritage of strength and confidence. Let's allow these early church leaders to inspire us; let's ask God to work in us as he worked in them; and let's step out in faith and see how God will use us, in our time, to reach others.

With God's help, let's lean toward greater boldness.

2. Get to the Central Message of the Gospel

Having said all of that, we need to not just be bold in bringing up spiritual topics of discussion—we need to remain bold enough to turn those conversations, when it seems appropriate and as the Holy Spirit leads, to the central message of the gospel.

Paul said, "For I am not ashamed of the gospel, because it is the power of God that brings salvation to everyone who believes: first to the Jew, then to the Gentile" (Romans 1:16). It's tempting to talk about spiritual matters in a broad and general way, but then to stop short of getting to the core message of the Christian faith, the gospel. But, as Paul so compellingly explains, *that's where the power is.*

Now, I'm not saying we must get to that central message in every spiritual conversation. Often, especially at the beginning, it's enough to just drop a hint, to mention something you're learning through the Bible, to extend an invitation to your church or discussion group, to answer a few spiritual questions. As we've been saying, evangelism is a process—and we are wise not to rush that process too much.

But may I instill a little *impatience* as well? We need to be mission-driven in our interactions, remembering that it's ultimately the message of the death and resurrection of Christ on our behalf that we must get to—and we don't have unlimited time and opportunities to do so. Therefore we should be prayerful and vigilant in our pursuit of those deeper interactions in which we can talk about the payment Jesus made on the cross for our sins, and the salvation he offers, and how his grace is available to anyone who will reach out to receive it—them included.

So be persistent in pressing toward the goal of discussing those core truths, but be patient in the process of getting there. And ask God to lead you to find the right balance of persistence and patience along the way.

3. Ask People to Respond to the Gospel

Once you've gotten to the point of discussing the central message of the gospel with your friends, don't stop there either! Instead, sustain your Holy Spirit-infused courage and take it one more step: ask them if they'd like to *respond* to that message.

The apostle Paul urges us, "Be wise in the way you act toward outsiders; make the most of every opportunity" (Colossians 4:5). Making the most of the opportunity, in many cases, entails not only telling them about God's gracious offer of salvation, but also asking them if they'd like to receive that salvation!

There's an old saying that tells us, "Evangelism is simply one beggar telling another beggar where to find bread." I like that. It reminds us that we are not better or smarter or more deserving than the other person—we're just fortunate enough to have received a great spiritual blessing, along with the privilege of sharing it with others.

But can you imagine a beggar telling other beggars that there really is a supply of bread available yet not telling them how to get it? It's not enough just to talk about what could be theirs—we need to help them receive it. Well, the same is true in evangelism. Far too often we simply talk about salvation but stop short of actually offering it to the other person.

Let's not do that anymore. Whether in one discussion or a series of conversations, let's make sure we get to the point of explaining how they can receive the gift of God's forgiveness, leadership, and the eternal life he offers them. And for those who are ready, let's go the final step of walking them across the line of faith to put their trust in Jesus. Sometimes you might need to give them a loving challenge to get off the spiritual fence they've been sitting on for so long. Often it's the nudge of a loving friend who will help people begin moving meaningfully toward Christ.

> How can we do that? In the next chapter we'll explain what the core message of the gospel is; we'll describe several ways we can illustrate that gospel to others; and we'll talk about how we can lead those who are ready in a prayer of commitment to Christ.

Cautions Concerning the *Truth-Telling* Style

Seek God's Guidance and Wisdom

Because of the strength of personality that often goes with this approach, it's important to seek wisdom from God (James 1:5), along with the gentleness and respect that Peter prescribes (1 Peter 3:15). It's also important to heed the biblical admonition to "be quick to listen, slow to speak and slow to become angry" (James 1:19). If you come on too strong or too fast, people will likely become defensive and distrust whatever you say.

So, slow down a bit. Seek the guidance and, as needed, the tempering of the Holy Spirit. Listen first, and once you're confident you understand the person's point of view and have earned their trust, then tell them the truth you think God wants them to hear. Expect that their first response may not be to thoughtfully consider what you've said or to thank you for sharing your wisdom. Even with your best efforts to communicate respectfully, many will resist what you're saying, and some will be offended by it.

Remember that many turned away from the teachings of Jesus, the Son of God himself. The same happened with Peter and with Paul, whose listeners often debated their ideas and, in the end, discarded what they had heard. Jesus cautioned us that just as people rejected him, they will often reject us.

But not all of them will reject us. Many are fed up with their hollow lives of endless striving, empty pleasure, or feigned religion. They're looking for something real. They're seeking rest for their souls, and relief from their guilt and moral bankruptcy. They're looking for Jesus and the truth of the gospel—but many of them don't know it yet.

We have the unspeakable privilege of offering it to them—of offering *him* to them. So, under God's guidance, keep patiently reaching out with his love and truth.

Resist Being Overly Cautious

This leads me to the next concern, which is to resist becoming *overly* cautious. Our culture has become hypersensitive, with many people thinking that the most offensive thing you can do is tell them they're wrong or try to change their mind (as, ironically, they try to tell us *we're* wrong and that we need to change *our* minds). Even among those who identify as Christians, many think it's inappropriate to try to convince someone to change their point of view in order to turn and follow Christ. Yet the kindest thing we can do for our friends is to help them understand there is a loving God who wants to redeem and renew their lives—*if* they turn to him in repentance and faith.

Remember the penetrating words of atheist Penn Gillette: "If you believe that there's a heaven and a hell . . . how much do you have to hate somebody to *not* proselytize?" As Paul said, "*Christ's love compels us*, because we are convinced that one died for all, and therefore all died. And he died for all, that those who live should no longer live for themselves but for him who died for them and was raised again" (2 Corinthians 5:14–15, emphasis mine).

Our priority, then, should not be to try to keep friendships smooth and tranquil at all costs, or to avoid ever offending anyone. Rather, it should be to "speak the truth in love" (Ephesians 4:15) in order to help secure the salvation and spiritual health of those we care about, even if the truth stings a little in the process. God's love should compel us to tell them about him and his grace, available in Christ.

We shouldn't be afraid, therefore, to occasionally make people feel uncomfortable—it comes with the territory of the *Truth-Telling* style. Again, don't unnecessarily offend anyone, but be willing to accept some level of uneasiness in others as a by-product of sharing the truth with them. Like Jesus did. And Peter. And "Yankee," Uncle Jack, and Greg Stier.

Affirm the Other Styles

One more word of caution. Once you've developed this style and God has used you to nudge people toward him, be careful not to project your approach onto other Christians, making them feel bad for not exhibiting the same level of boldness as you. Remember there are at least five different approaches to sharing our faith. *You be you*, and *let them be them*, and trust God to use all the members of his body in partnership with each other.

The Extraordinary Impact of Spiritual Truth-Telling

I was raised in a Christian home, but when I was nineteen years old I was not walking with God. I was clearly on the wrong track in my life, seeking fun and adventure, even when it meant coloring outside of the lines morally. I knew what was right, but throughout my high school years and beyond I had resisted it and gone my own way. I needed a spiritual challenge from a *Truth-Telling* friend.

Then one day Terry, a guy I'd known since middle school, entered the electronics shop where I worked. After pretending to be interested in a car stereo, he got to his real point: "So, Mark, are you a Christian?"

His simple question was quite intimidating at the time. "Sure, I'm a Christian, Terry. What about it?" I replied warily.

Terry responded with another question: "How can you call yourself a Christian and yet do so many things that Christians don't do?"

"Well," I said flippantly, "I guess I'm just a *cool* Christian!"

Without batting an eye, Terry shot back, "Oh, really? Don't you know that there's a word for 'cool Christians'?" I shook my head, though Terry wasn't really waiting for a reply. "They're called hypocrites!"

Ouch.

I was not very receptive to this challenge and managed to end the conversation fairly quickly, but even after Terry left, his words lingered. At first I felt angry, but I soon realized why: I knew that Terry was *right!*

Gradually my anger turned into reflection, and within a few days that reflection turned into repentance. Finally, about a week later, I committed my life to Christ. That decision changed the trajectory of my life, and it put me on an unexpected adventure unlike anything I'd ever experienced before.

No, the *Truth-Telling* style is not my main approach. But I thank God for people like Terry—and perhaps like you—who have the personality and courage to speak truth where it's needed most. Because that's what it took to wake me up spiritually, and I'll be thanking him for all of eternity.

AN EPIDEMIC OF SPIRITUAL INFLUENCE

In his bestselling book, *The Tipping Point*, Malcolm Gladwell compares the spread of ideas to *epidemics,* and he explains that all epidemics have three common characteristics. "One, contagiousness; two, the fact that little causes can have big effects; and three, that change happens not gradually but at one dramatic moment . . . The name given to that one dramatic moment in an epidemic when everything can change all at once is the Tipping Point."[1]

Let's look briefly at these characteristics in the context of what we've been discussing.

One, *contagiousness.* The kind of faith we've been describing is by its very definition *contagious,* because of the kinds of elements presented in the first chapter. These include that it is fueled by love; that it is based on truth; that we must authentically have it before we can give it to others; and that it is spiritually empowered by the living God. Also, the gospel message itself is filled with grace, hope, forgiveness, and the promise of new life. These elements and many more make it highly attractive.

Two, *little causes can have big effects.* I trust you've been inspired by the five *Contagious Faith Styles* and the *Key Skills for Every Christian.* As the stories illustrate, there's incredible potential in followers of Christ realizing which approach best fits them, taking steps to put that approach into action, and—with the power of the Holy Spirit—sharing Jesus with others. More than that, I hope you've now discovered your primary style or maybe a combination of two or three of them—or perhaps you are style number six or seven that I haven't thought of. And I pray that you're feeling increasingly unleashed to develop and deploy it to reach others for Christ.

Three, *change happens at one dramatic moment.* As you take more and more Spirit-guided risks for the sake of friends who need God's grace and truth, you'll increasingly see that Paul was right when he called the gospel "the power of God that brings salvation to everyone who believes" (Romans 1:16). How does he describe the changes this salvation brings? "This means that anyone who belongs to Christ has become a new person," Paul explains. "The old life is gone; a new life has begun!" (2 Corinthians 5:17). Talk about change happening both dramatically and quickly!

And just wait until you experience the synergism that happens when you start to intentionally team up with other believers who have different styles than you do. When you learn to effectively partner with each other and with God in reaching out to your family and friends, and when you take God-honoring risks to do whatever it takes to reach them, then you'll begin to experience an epidemic of contagious Christian influence in your wider circle of acquaintances. You'll become part of the exciting spiritual tipping point that is already happening in some parts of the world, but which needs to happen in much greater measure right here at home.

In the book's final section, we'll unpack the powerful message of the gospel and ways we can effectively explain it. Then we'll explore what we can do when our style doesn't seem to fit certain evangelistic opportunities. Finally, we'll discuss the importance of taking risks for the sake of the gospel, and we'll see how all of this can culminate in our leaving a lasting spiritual legacy.

CHAPTER 8

UNDERSTANDING AND APPLYING THE GOSPEL

For I am not ashamed of the gospel, because
it is the power of God that brings salvation to
everyone who believes: first to the Jew, then to
the Gentile.

—ROMANS 1:16

I saw the mail truck heading our way today, so I walked down the driveway to pick up our delivery. The postal worker that Heidi and I have been getting to know for a few years, who I'll call Rosemary, handed me several letters while telling me she had a question.

"Great, what is it?" I replied, as I silently asked God for wisdom.

"I've been wondering," she began. "How can we know that we've really done all we need to do in order to be okay with God?"

This was the continuation of a couple of other short

interactions we'd had over the past year or so, and I'd recently given her a small evangelistic book I'd written called *The Reason Why Faith Makes Sense*, so I wasn't completely surprised that she brought up the topic.

"That's a really good question," I said, gathering my thoughts quickly, knowing she was on a tight schedule to finish her route. "There's an illustration that I think helps provide a good answer, and I'll explain it briefly because I know you don't have a lot of time." I proceeded to describe the *Do vs. Done* illustration that you'll read about later in this chapter.

I explained that we can't make ourselves "okay with God" through a bunch of religious activities, going to church, or doing good deeds—even though those can all be positive things. I said that such an approach plays into the *DO* plan of trying to perform enough good works in order to try to pay off our bad deeds and earn our way to God. "That plan never succeeds," I went on, "because the Bible makes it clear in Romans 3:23 that no matter how much we do, our efforts always fall short of God's perfect standard.

"Instead," I continued, "we need to humbly admit to God that we've sinned against him and can't ever do enough to work our way back to him. Rather, we need to give up on our own efforts and put our faith in Jesus and what he has already *DONE* for us by dying on the cross to pay the penalty for our sins. Having a right relationship with God will never happen through what we *do*—it comes through putting our trust in what Christ has *done* for us, and by following him.

"I should add, though, that it's not enough to just know this. We need to respond to what Jesus has done for us, by asking him to give us his salvation and by telling him we want to give him our life from this day forward, making him our forgiver and leader. That's what I did when I was nineteen years old, and it completely changed my life."

"Well, I think I get that—" Rosemary responded, as her cellphone started ringing. "I mean, I think I'm doing everything I can to be a better Christian."

I smiled as she turned off her phone, and I gently pointed out that "doing everything I can" still sounded a lot like the *DO* plan. I explained again that our religious efforts will always fail, so we need to come to the end of our spiritual rope and then let go of it—giving up our reliance on anything we can ever do to get back to God. And I urged her, instead, to make sure she embraces Jesus and what he has *DONE* for us by dying for our sins and rising to give us new life.

She assured me she would and that she'd keep reading the book I'd given her, adding that we could talk about it again soon. And after that two-or three-minute exchange she was off to deliver the mail to our neighbors.

I said a prayer for Rosemary as she drove away, and hope that soon she'll come to the point of real trust and confidence in what Jesus has done for her.

Getting Ready

A recurring theme in this book—and in Scripture—is that we need to get ready to talk to people about our faith and then seize opportunities when they open up, whether we feel ready or not. Peter said to "be prepared" (1 Peter 3:15). Paul said to "be wise in the way you act toward outsiders," and "make the most of every opportunity" (Colossians 4:5). He added in his interactions with Timothy to "be prepared in season and out of season" (2 Timothy 4:2).

Was I prepared for my brief conversation with Rosemary? Honestly, I'd have to say yes . . . and no.

Yes, in the sense that I knew and was able to explain an illustration that helps delineate between the works mentality many people in our culture have versus the biblical message of salvation made available through the work of Christ. I was glad I had a conversational tool like that ready, and I would encourage you to master a few like it as well.

No, in the sense that I was not expecting an opportunity to open up so suddenly during a routine stroll to the mailbox, and I was caught a bit off guard. I had to collect and express my thoughts almost instantly, in spite of feeling pretty "out of season" in that particular moment.

As I walked back to the house a few minutes later, I was glad I'd said what I'd said, but I also felt a sense of inadequacy— knowing that so much more could and should be explained. Did I say enough about what it means to really know Jesus as a person? To follow him as our God and King? Words often seem deficient when trying to summarize the difference between dead religious activity and a vibrant relationship with our living Savior.

Thankfully, the Holy Spirit is able to take our imperfect efforts and apply them to people's hearts and minds in perfect ways. And, hopefully, I'll have more opportunities soon to tell Rosemary more of the story.

How about you—do you think you'd feel ready in a similar situation? My guess is that you, like me, can always use more preparation in order to be sure you're ready to "make the most of every opportunity" that comes your way. That's the goal of this chapter—to help us get clear on what the gospel message really is, and then to learn some ways we can illustrate it succinctly next time someone looks at us and says, "I've got a question for you."

The Story of Jesus

The gospel *seems* pretty straightforward. Every Christian knows the message and ought to be able to communicate it in short order, right? Well, think again. This is actually the subject of a lot of spirited discussion today among theologians and New Testament scholars. Of these, I found the insights of Scot McKnight particularly helpful, especially in his book, *The King Jesus Gospel: The Original Good News Revisited*.[1]

Here's the upshot: much of what we now call the gospel is not what Jesus and his apostles called the gospel. Often what people now refer to as the gospel is actually a narrower salvation message. That message is important, but it's a subset of the larger story that the New Testament preachers presented and that God used to change the world.

Why does this matter? Because the focus of the biblical gospel is *Jesus*—who he is, what he came to do, what he accomplished through his death and resurrection, and how we can respond by becoming part of his kingdom by trusting and following him as our Lord and King. Jesus is the epicenter of the gospel, and it, by its very nature, is designed to produce *disciples of Jesus*. And it is this gospel message that he commissioned every one of us as his followers to deliver throughout the world (Matthew 28:18–20), and which Paul describes as "the power of God that brings salvation to everyone who believes" (Romans 1:16).

But the focus of the narrower salvation message is *us*— what our problem is (sin), what God's solution is (Jesus's death on the cross), and what our response should be (trust in Jesus). This message, when presented in isolation from the larger gospel story, often produces spiritual *decisions* but not necessarily Christian *disciples*. Why? Because people can end up with the misguided idea that we're offering them a plan for superficial self-improvement (with God's help), rather than the opportunity to humbly turn from their sins to receive the salvation of the Savior and the guidance of the King.

We see the flawed fruit of this reductionistic message all around us, with many people saying they are Christians simply because they "prayed a prayer," or "went forward at a meeting," or "were baptized at church"—even though their lives may not reflect biblical values or the leadership of Jesus. Their attitude is that they have checked the right box in order to get the desired benefit. As a result, false conversions abound, and many self-described believers don't really know who Jesus is or what they were supposedly signing up for.

Now, don't get me wrong. I'm all for calling people to respond to Christ, to pray prayers of faith and repentance, and to be baptized as believers. But they need to do these things in the context of the broader gospel message. The biblical pattern is that we should tell the story about Jesus, including who he is and the mission he came to accomplish, and within that context explain how people can respond to him appropriately.

What We Need to Know: Understanding the Gospel

What is the gospel? The introduction to Mark, the earliest biography or "Gospel" of Jesus, introduces the gospel message by saying, "The beginning of the good news about Jesus the

Messiah, the Son of God . . ." (Mark 1:1). The focus of Mark's message was on *Jesus*, who was, first, the long-awaited Messiah, the royal figure predicted in the Old Testament—the anointed King who would come through the lineage of King David (Isaiah 9:6–7; Jeremiah 23:5–6; Matthew 1:1)—and second, the unique Son of God, which the Bible makes clear was a description of deity—a divine person (the one who theologians would later describe as the second person of the Trinity. See Isaiah 9:6–7; Daniel 7:13–14; Mark 14:61–63; John 5:16–18; John 8:56–59; John 10:25–33; and John 20:26–29).

A few verses later Mark adds that "Jesus went into Galilee, proclaiming the good news of God. 'The time has come,' [Jesus] said. 'The kingdom of God has come near. Repent and believe the good news!'" (Mark 1:14–15). Jesus was affirming that through him, the prophesied King, the kingdom of God had arrived— and that this information was at least the beginning of the Good News, the gospel.

Later, after Jesus's crucifixion and resurrection, Peter and the other disciples waited for the Holy Spirit, whom Jesus had promised, to come upon them. Then, after being filled with and empowered by God's Spirit, Peter stood up on the Day of Pentecost and boldly preached to the crowd that had gathered in Jerusalem. He said, "Let all Israel be assured of this: God has made this Jesus, whom you crucified, both *Lord* and *Messiah*" (Acts 2:36, emphases mine). This was shorthand for saying: *The one who died and rose was, in reality, the God of the universe and the long-awaited King of Israel (and, ultimately, of the entire world).*

The apostle Paul introduced the same core message at the beginning of his letter to the Romans. He referred to it as "the gospel of God—the gospel he promised beforehand through his prophets in the Holy Scriptures regarding his Son, who as to his earthly life was a descendant of David, and who through the Spirit of holiness was appointed the Son of God in power by his resurrection from the dead: Jesus Christ our Lord" (Romans 1:1–4). Again, in short, Paul was announcing: *Jesus is both our predicted royal King and our God.*

Paul echoes this again in his brief statement in 2 Timothy 2:8, "Remember Jesus Christ, raised from the dead, descended from David. This is my gospel." Keep in mind that "Jesus" is his name, and "Christ" is his title, which is the Greek translation of the Hebrew word "Messiah," which means "anointed King."[2] So Paul is saying: *Focus on Jesus, the anointed King (who, as prophesied, is the descendant of King David), who proved his deity by rising from the dead.*

Paul also presents what many consider the Bible's most detailed summary of the gospel in 1 Corinthians 15:3–5, where he quotes the first creed of the church, which goes right back to the time of the events themselves. In fact, eminent New Testament scholar James D. G. Dunn says we can be entirely confident that this creed was formulated *within months* of Jesus's death.[3]

Paul previews this creed with an introduction: "Now, brothers and sisters, I want to remind you of the gospel I preached to you, which you received and on which you have taken your stand. By this gospel you are saved, if you hold firmly to the word I preached to you. Otherwise, you have believed in vain" (verses 1–2). Note how emphatically Paul announces: *This is the real gospel—accept it and don't mess with it!* (Also see his stern warning against substituting other messages for the genuine gospel in Galatians 1:8–10.)

Paul continues in 1 Corinthians 15:3: "For what I received I passed on to you as of first importance." This was code for: here's the creed that was officially formulated by the apostles who were there, previously handed down to me, and I now pass it on to you as the top priority.

Next Paul gives us the actual content of the creed, which summarizes the central gospel message: "That Christ died for our sins according to the Scriptures, that he was buried, that he was raised on the third day according to the Scriptures, and that he appeared to Cephas [the Aramaic name for Peter], and then to the Twelve" (verses 3–5). Paul adds these confirming details: "After that, he appeared to more than five hundred of the brothers and sisters at the same time, most of whom are still living, though some have fallen asleep. Then he appeared to James, then to all the apostles, and last of all he appeared to me also . . ." (verses 6–8).

McKnight makes a strong case that, after addressing a few other concerns, Paul comes back to complete his gospel message in verses 20–28. "In other words," McKnight explains, "there are reasons to think the gospel of Paul included the ascension of Jesus, the second coming of Christ, and the full consummation of the kingdom when God becomes all in all."[4] This seems right to me, both from the context and because it completes the story of Jesus and his divine mission.

To summarize, then, here are the main points of the gospel:[5]

- Jesus, the Messiah and Lord (the long-awaited King of Israel and incarnate God of the universe), came to our sinful and fallen planet, bringing God's kingdom (verse 3; Mark 1:15; Acts 2:36).

- King Jesus was rejected and condemned, and he died a criminal's death for us—the spiritual criminals—and our sins, as predicted (verse 3; Isaiah 53; Philippians 2:8; 1 Peter 3:18).
- Jesus was really dead, and his body was buried in a tomb (verses 3–4).
- Three days later Jesus was raised back to life, as prophesied (verse 4; Isaiah 53:10–12; Psalm 16:9–11, also predicted by Jesus in all four Gospels: Matthew 16:21; Mark 9:30–32; Luke 18:31–34; John 2:19–22). This proved that he was the royal Messiah and divine Son of God, who conquered death.
- The resurrected Jesus appeared to his disciples and many others (verses 5–8), proving he truly was alive again, that he is who he claimed to be, and that he is able to give us new life.
- Jesus ascended into heaven, returning to the Father until he comes back again to bring salvation to his people and judgment to those who reject him, and to establish his kingdom forever (verses 20–28).

Let me add a note about the recurring theme throughout these passages—that this long-awaited Messiah would be the royal *King* over God's kingdom. It's hard to find a modern term that does justice to the concept people had in their minds during biblical times. I know that for me, and maybe for you, the word *king* takes me either to some earlier time in history that I don't really relate to, or to a fictional story like *The Lord of the Rings*. Or even to current cultures where the king or a queen are mere symbolic figureheads. None of these begin to do justice to what was being announced concerning Jesus in the gospel proclamations.

I've tried and failed to think of a singular term that encompasses all of the right elements today. The closest I've come is to imagine a combination of a great nation's *president*, its top *military commander*, and its wisest *scholar*—and none of that includes the part about him being the *Lord of the Universe!* Wrap all of that together and you only *begin* to get a sense of what Peter meant when he announced to the crowd in Acts 2:36, "Therefore let all Israel be assured of this: God has made this Jesus, whom you crucified, both Lord and Messiah."

Our appropriate response to the gospel is not only to put our trust in the message by faith, but also to shift our loyalty away from any other sovereign that has been in our life (including ourselves) in order to follow and give our sole allegiance to this royal King, Jesus.[6] Paul emphasized the *faith* aspect in this well-known passage: "For it is by grace you have been saved, through faith— and this is not from yourselves, it is the gift of God" (Ephesians 2:8). And in Lystra, Paul and Barnabas punctuated the *allegiance* part when they declared, "We are bringing you good news, telling you to turn from these worthless things to the living God, who made the heavens and the earth and the sea and everything in them" (Acts 14:15). Paul also described true followers of Christ as those who had "turned to God from idols to serve the living and true God" (1 Thessalonians 1:9).

In short, as the old hymn puts it, we need to:

> *Trust and obey, for there's no other way*
> *To be happy in Jesus, but to trust and obey.*

What We Need to Do: Illustrating and Applying the Gospel

Now that we've explored the message of the biblical gospel, let's move on to the practical question of how we can effectively explain, illustrate, and apply it in the lives of the people we talk to.

1. Talk through the Gospel Story

Generally speaking, we'll best reflect the biblical pattern and better serve people if we find opportunities to slow down and really *talk to them*. Tell the story of Jesus. Explain who he is. Unpack the reasons he came to earth and what he accomplished. And *then* describe how they should respond to that message.

Here's a succinct outline of the gospel:

1. Jesus, the incarnate Son of God and predicted King, came to our fallen planet;
2. he died for our sins;
3. he was buried;
4. he rose on the third day;
5. he appeared to many witnesses;
6. he returned to heaven until he comes back to judge his enemies and establish his eternal kingdom with us, his followers.

It is to this story and this Savior that people need to respond with faith and allegiance.

This is the essential message that the apostles preached, and we can share it with our friends in a conversational way, whether in one talk or over multiple discussions. It forms the biblical framework for all the other illustrations below.

2. Illustrate the Gospel and Explain How People Need to Respond to It

With the backdrop of the broader gospel story established, we can now look at a variety of ways to illustrate the gospel as well as the appropriate response to it. I'll present several different illustrations, since some people will relate better to one than another. Also, you might find that a specific approach best helps in addressing a particular area of confusion that your friend is wrestling with.

The Faith Formula

This illustration is drawn from John 1:12.[7] The passage immediately preceding that verse explains that most of the world had rejected Jesus, but then verse 12 says, "Yet to all who did receive him, to those who believed in his name, he gave the right to become children of God."

There are three active verbs in that verse: *believe, receive*, and *become*. Put into the Faith Formula, they look like this:

$$\text{BELIEVE} + \text{RECEIVE} = \text{BECOME}$$

What does it mean? Simply this: we must *Believe* the gospel story about Jesus—that he is the Son of God who came to earth, died on the cross to pay for our sins, and rose from the dead to give us life. More than that, we need to *Receive* Jesus for who he claims to be—our Savior and King. When we sincerely do that, the verse says we *Become* a child of God. We're forgiven and adopted into his family!

This is one of my favorite illustrations due to its simplicity and because it emphasizes the fact that it's not enough to just nod our heads in agreement with a biblical message or gospel sermon (as so many people mistakenly assume). Yes, we do need to agree with it, but we also need to explicitly put our trust in the content of that message and receive the divine person the message is about—Jesus, our forgiver and leader.

The Airplane Illustration

Building on the Faith Formula (and the overarching gospel story), here's another illustration I often use in explaining how we should respond to the gospel:

Let's say a family member offers to fly you home for the holidays. It's a great offer but getting home will require two things. First, you have to *believe* that airplanes fly. You'll never be willing to get on one if you don't believe it will really get you over the mountains, right?

But just believing that airplanes fly won't get you home either. You can be fully confident in the science of flight, even hang around an airport and watch planes take off and land. But it takes more than belief in aviation to get home. You must also *receive* the ticket that was purchased for you and use it to board the airplane that is heading to your hometown. It's that combination of believing and receiving that allows you to *become* a passenger on that flight who will, as a result, get back home.

It is much the same with Christ. We need to go beyond merely *Believing* that Jesus is the Son of God who died on the cross for our sins and who rose to give us life. We must take the next step and trust in him personally, *Receiving* him as the forgiver of our sins and the leader of our lives. That is the equivalent of "climbing on board" with Jesus in a way that will ultimately get us home spiritually, where we *Become* his forgiven sons and daughters.[8]

Romans 10:9–10

"If you declare with your mouth, 'Jesus is Lord,' and believe in your heart that God raised him from the dead, you will be saved. For it is with your heart that you believe and are justified, and it is with your mouth that you profess your faith and are saved" (Romans 10:9–10).

This passage was a favorite of my late friend Nabeel Qureshi, a former Muslim. In his final book, *No God But One*, he asks "What defines Christianity at its core . . . ?" Then he points to Romans 10:9 and says that we find in it "the entire gospel message formulated as the minimum requirement for saving faith. It has three components: (1) that Jesus died, (2) that he rose from the dead, and (3) that he is God."[9] Nabeel would often sum that up with these three words: *Deity, Death,* and *Resurrection.*

So, Jesus is the God who can save us, the Savior who died for our sins, and the Risen Lord who can give us new life. But what are we to do with these truths? Verse 10 tells us to believe them in our heart and profess our trust in them with our mouth (which sounds a lot like the John 1:12 formula of Believe + Receive, but with the added element that we should declare this verbally). When we do so sincerely, according to verse 10, we are *justified* (made right with God) and *saved* (given God's salvation). As if to punctuate this promise, a few verses later we're assured that "everyone who calls on the name of the Lord will be saved" (Romans 10:13).

Do vs. Done

This simple illustration focuses on how we need to *respond* to the Good News of the gospel. It exposes the inadequacy of our human tendency to try to earn God's favor, and it shows that salvation can only be obtained by trusting in Christ and his substitutionary work for us on the cross.

I used a modified version of this with our mail delivery woman, Rosemary, as I described at the beginning of this chapter. Here's how I usually explain it:

Would you like to know the difference between religion and Christianity? It's in how they are *spelled!*

Religion is spelled "D-O" [it's helpful to write down the word "DO"]. It consists of trying to *do* enough good things to earn our way back to God. The problem is we never know when we have done enough. Worse than that, the Bible makes it clear that we never *can* do enough. (Romans 3:23 says: "For all have sinned and fall short of the glory of God.")

Christianity, on the other hand, is spelled "D-O-N-E" [if you're writing, add to your previous "DO" the letters "NE," completing the word, DONE]. That's because Jesus has lovingly and willingly *done* for us what we could never do for ourselves. He lived the perfect life that we could never live. Then he died on the cross to pay for all of our sins, and he rose from the dead to offer us new life.

But it is not enough to just know or agree with this. We have to receive him and what he has DONE for us. We do that by turning from our old ways and humbly asking him for his forgiveness and leadership in our lives—making him our Savior, God, and King.

3. Help Friends Respond to the Gospel

Our goal should be more than simply sharing this information with our friends. Our aim should be to help them put their trust in Christ. Therefore, as we're talking through our testimonies, answering their questions, or explaining the gospel message, we should prayerfully seek to discern if they are beginning to open up to him.

When you see that starting to happen, it's wise to test the situation. You can gently ask them questions like these: *"Is this making sense to you?"* *"What do you think about what I've shared?"* *"Does it raise any questions in your mind?"* Such inquiries can deepen the conversation quickly. And when you sense that your friend is becoming receptive to what you've been discussing, it's often appropriate to finally just come out and ask them, *"Is there any reason you wouldn't want to put your trust in Jesus right now?"*

I like this question because more often than you might expect it will evoke a positive answer. "Honestly," they might say, "I think I've been holding out on God long enough." Or they may reply, "Well, I'd like to—but I really don't know what to do." When you get that kind of an open response, don't delay. Explain that this is something they can do right now by praying and asking for Jesus to become their forgiver and leader.

Specifically, ask them to pray with you in their own words, out loud (and without trying to sound religious). Tell them you'll start the prayer, and then prompt them in a few areas that they can talk to God about.

What areas? Here are three words that sum up what our main response should be: *Turn, Trust,* and *Follow.*

1. **Turn**—we need to confess and turn away—or repent—from our sin, self-rule, and false idols (Mark 1:15; Acts 2:38; Acts 26:20; 1 Thessalonians 1:9; 1 John 1:9).
2. **Trust**—we need to put our faith in Jesus as our forgiver, or Savior, who died on the cross for our sins (Romans 1:17; Ephesians 2:8–9, 1 Corinthians 15:3).

3. **Follow**—we must commit to following Jesus as our leader, God, and King (we shift our allegiance to him and become his faithful servant), under the power of his Holy Spirit who now comes to live within us (Acts 1:8; Romans 8:2, 9–11; Ephesians 5:18).

Specifically, I would start the prayer by thanking God for my friend's openness, and I would ask God to lead them as they pray to receive Christ. Then, with heads bowed, I'd prompt my friend to talk to God in their own words, expressing their desire to *Turn* from their old sinful patterns, alliances, and pride [and pause to let them do so]; then to express their *Trust* in Jesus and his finished work on the cross to pay for their sins [again pausing to let them pray]; and finally to acknowledge their desire to *Follow* Jesus as their leader and King from this day forward with the help of the Holy Spirit, who will now begin to indwell and empower them [pause for them to pray once more]. Finally, I'd close by thanking God for what he just began to do in my friend's life. Then I'd say "Amen" and congratulate my friend for taking the most important step they could ever take!

I'd then explain to them that this is really just their spiritual *birth*—the beginning of this new life with God. But now there needs to be spiritual growth in the days, weeks, and years ahead. I would make sure they have a Bible in a translation they can understand, and urge them to start reading it each day, beginning in the New Testament. I'd also coach them to start praying honestly and regularly to their Savior, leader, and friend.

Also, I'd urge them to tell others about their newfound faith right away—including believers who will encourage them in it, as well as nonbelievers who might be reached through it. Yes, get them started with sharing Jesus with others as soon as possible. Newer Christians often have a highly contagious faith—and sharing it with others will help reinforce their commitment to it!

In addition, I'd be sure to help them find a solid, gospel-centered church in their area as soon as possible, where they can be baptized as a new believer, and where they can learn, grow, and get regular encouragement in their walk with Christ. These initial steps might seem simple, but they're vitally important elements of their ongoing spiritual growth.

On the other hand, when we check to see if our friends are open to trusting in Christ right now, their answer will often be "no" or "not yet." But there's another reason I like to ask this pointed question—because it will help you (and them) diagnose their situation. They might reply, "I'm interested, but I have too many unanswered questions." Then you can try to find out what those questions are, help them weigh the importance of those matters and, where needed, help them discover good answers. Or they may say, "I really can't right now because, honestly, I have a few things in my life that I'm not ready to give up." But if they'll open up about the nature of those things, you can help them assess how valuable they really are compared to the many surpassing benefits of knowing Christ, both in this life and the next.

Finally, as we mentioned earlier, you might need to give them a loving nudge to get out of spiritual neutral and to embrace the amazing gift of grace that God is offering them. Often, it's the challenge of a caring friend that will help people finally step across the line of faith and put their trust in Christ.

Infectious Impact

Regardless of what your primary *Contagious Faith Style* (or styles) might be, what you do through that approach needs to lead ultimately to the point where you can share the life-changing message of the gospel with your friend.

Maybe you're the *Friendship-Building* style, so you bring up the gospel message after having several meals and conversations together. Or the *Selfless-Serving* style, and after serving your friend in some way you ask if you can explain the message that changed your life and turned you into someone who likes to help others. Maybe you have the *Story-Sharing* style, so after telling them your story you ask if you can explain in a bit more depth what was really the pivotal turning point of your life. Or you have the *Reason-Giving* style, so after explaining some of the evidence that supports your faith, you offer to outline the main idea that all this information leads to—an idea that has changed countless lives. Or, finally, if you have the *Truth-Telling* style, you can offer to explain the most important truth you've ever heard—one you think could change everything for them.

Combining your natural approach with the supernatural message of the gospel is a powerful combination that God can use to impact your friend's life and future in ways that are hard to fully comprehend. Put these ideas into action, and your faith will become truly contagious.

CHAPTER 9

WHEN YOUR STYLE DOESN'T FIT THE SITUATION

What, after all, is Apollos? And what is Paul?
Only servants, through whom you came to
believe—as the Lord has assigned to each his
task. I planted the seed, Apollos watered it, but
God has been making it grow.

—1 CORINTHIANS 3:5-6

I barely noticed the guy behind the counter as I breezed into the ice cream shop that evening. I was too focused on finding the sign listing the flavor of the day. But my friend Karl saw the man. I had just identified the flavor of the day as White Chocolate Mousse when I heard Karl say to him, "Based on your appearance and accent, I'm guessing you're from somewhere in the Middle East. So I'm curious: Are you a Muslim or a Christian?"

Karl is a straight-shooting, hard-hitting, type-A entrepreneur who buys and sells businesses as casually as most of us change socks. He is highly successful and accustomed to being in charge. He also loves God and people passionately—and is constantly looking for ways to introduce them to each other. Karl is a classic example of the *Truth-Telling* style. He doesn't like small talk but prefers to get to the point. He enjoys stirring up action—even if that means striking up a faith-based conversation with the stranger behind an ice cream counter.

I held my breath, wondering if Rocky Road would be a more appropriate choice for the flavor of the day.

"That's an interesting question," the man replied. "I grew up in a Muslim country and was raised in the Islamic faith. But I've been in America for a couple of years, and I've met some great Christians. I don't know what to think—I guess I'm somewhere in the middle right now, trying to figure out what to believe."

"That's fascinating," Karl said, as he quickly got the man's name and motioned for me to come closer. Karl knew that my preferred approach to evangelism is the *Reason-Giving* style, and since I was just in town for a visit, he was trying to make the most of the opportunity.

"Mark, I'd like you to meet my new friend, Fayz. And Fayz, this is Mark; he likes to study these kinds of topics." As we met, Karl turned to me and added, "Fayz wants to know more about Jesus, and why we trust in him instead of in Muhammad."

He does? I thought to myself—probably at the same split-second that Fayz thought to himself, *I do?*

Gulp. Forget the ice cream!

I was surprised to be so quickly immersed in a discussion about the ins and outs of Islam and Christianity, but I did my best. I tried to succinctly explain the distinctions between our faiths, but kept getting interrupted by families coming in to order desserts.

"It's hard to go too deep right now," I finally conceded. "But a friend of mine wrote a book that relates to this topic. If you'd be willing to take a look at it, I'll bring you a copy."

Fayz politely agreed, so Karl and I bought our ice cream and found out when it would be best for us to come back.

A couple of days later we brought a copy of *The Case for Christ* to Fayz and urged him to read it. I was excited to see what Lee Strobel's mix of the *Story-Sharing* and *Reason-Giving* styles might do to help Fayz take spiritual steps forward. I was also happy to see that he was anticipating our return, and he seemed genuinely interested in Lee's book.

Karl didn't stop there, though. A week or two after I had finished my visit and flown back home, he returned to the ice cream shop with his wonderful wife Barbara. She is a great example of the *Friendship-Building* style because she's so adept at forming authentic relationships with people. She quickly befriended Fayz and found out that he had a wife and young daughter. Before long, the two families were getting together for meals.

It didn't stop there, either. Karl and Barbara were part of an adult class at their church, and they told the group about how they were reaching out to their new Muslim friend and his wife. They asked for prayer and encouraged their friends to do some evangelistic ice cream outings of their own. Almost instantly, God unleashed a hundred hungry Baptists on this unsuspecting Muslim!

Suddenly a variety of Christians were meeting Fayz, building friendships with him, inviting him to various events, sharing their testimonies, and addressing his spiritual questions. And when some members of the class discovered that Fayz was a medical student who was selling ice cream to pay his way through school, several of them employed the *Selfless-Serving* style by helping him make connections in the local medical community.

This band of believers was deploying all of the *Contagious Faith Styles* of evangelism—*Truth-Telling, Reason-Giving, Story-Sharing, Friendship-Building,* and *Selfless-Serving.* They were partnering powerfully in their efforts to lovingly reach out to this man and his family.

When Your Natural Approach Doesn't Fit the Need

It's a sobering reality that when you share your faith with others, sometimes you're going to feel out of your league, or perhaps just out of place. Mismatched. Even if you feel confident in telling people around you about Jesus, it will quickly become apparent that not everyone will relate to your natural style.

This can be discouraging. But remember that God knew what he was doing when he made you. You were, as the Bible reminds us, "fearfully and wonderfully made" (Psalm 139:14). This is not just true of you physically, but also spiritually and emotionally. *Your personality is on purpose.* God made you intentionally, with your unique mix, and I believe that he'll use you in ways that are congruent with that design. So go ahead and let God work through the real *you* by loving, serving, and reaching out to those he has placed in your world.

But what about situations when you realize you're reaching out to someone with whom you don't have a natural fit? This will sometimes be the case, whether due to your different personalities, backgrounds, stages of life, or a host of other factors. What should you do when you sense that you're not connecting in ways that will optimally help the other person in their spiritual journey? Give up? Walk away? Silently hand them over to the Lord, hoping *he'll* do something with them?

Let me share a couple of alternatives. When our natural approach isn't a great fit for the person or situation we find ourselves in, we can *partner* with other believers who will be a better fit. Or when necessary we can *stretch*, with God's help, giving him the chance to use us anyway.

And regardless of which direction we go, we always need to rely on the Holy Spirit, and trust him to work in and through us, making us partners with God in helping people take steps toward Christ. Let's examine these thoughts in a bit more depth.

Often We Need to Partner

Generally, as we discussed in chapter 1, we weren't meant to go solo in sharing Christ with others. In fact, Jesus, whose mission was "to seek and to save the lost" (Luke 19:10), selected a dozen people for his initial outreach team (Luke 6:12–16). And when he recruited seventy-two more, he sent them out in pairs (Luke 10). And then, right before he ascended back into heaven, he commissioned every believer to be part of his global team to make disciples around the world (Matthew 28:18–20). Yes, faith-sharing is meant to be a team effort.

In addition, Paul explains in 1 Corinthians: "There are different kinds of gifts, but the same Spirit distributes them. There are different kinds of service, but the same Lord. There are different kinds of working, but in all of them and in everyone it is the same God at work. Now to each one the manifestation of the Spirit is given for the common good" (1 Corinthians 12:4–7). Paul's main subject in this passage is spiritual gifts, but in it we see a broader principle—that God delights to work through "different kinds of service" and "different kinds of working," yet it's all "the same God at work . . . for the common good." This principle applies powerfully in the area of evangelism, as we've seen in the biblical examples of the five *Contagious Faith Styles*.

And when we learn to be intentional about partnering with other believers whose style will better fit the need than our own, the impact can expand rapidly. That's what we saw Karl do in the example above. He used his bold, *Truth-Telling* style to get the conversation going. But as soon as he recognized the need for expertise on Islam, he conscripted me with my *Reason-Giving* style into the conversation. We then tapped into Lee Strobel's *Story-Sharing* approach by giving Fayz Lee's book, and later Karl partnered with his wife Barbara's *Friendship-Building* style, and members of his church class jumped in and employed the *Selfless-Serving* style by helping Fayz make inroads into the local medical community.

This was the idea Heidi and I stumbled upon when we were going door to door in the neighborhoods of South London, learning to utilize the natural styles God had given each of us, but in tandem. We didn't have names for them at that time, but her *Friendship-Building* style helped open doors—literally—for my *Reason-Giving* style.

More recently, our different approaches worked together again when Heidi and I partnered to reach our neighbor Kathy after meeting her at our first Flamingo Party. What I didn't mention is that after Kathy received Christ, Heidi and I teamed up with Kathy to help lead her fiancé, Don, to faith as well. Then several of us partnered again to reach out to another friend of Kathy's in the neighborhood, Lynn—who had hosted the first

Flamingo Party we went to—and Lynn also put her trust in Christ.

Soon after that, some other neighbors opened their home, including their outdoor hot tub, so we could have a small baptism service. Kathy, Don, and Lynn shared short testimonies in front of family members, friends, and a few spiritually curious neighbors. Then I had the privilege of baptizing all three of them. [Later note: As I was putting the finishing touches on this book, Heidi met with Janine, one of the neighbors who had attended the baptism service, and had the privilege of clarifying the gospel and leading her in a prayer of commitment to Christ!]

We've seen a mini epidemic of contagious faith in our little subdivision. Why? Because God is working through an increasing number of Christians who are partnering together in ways that fit each of us, all in order to bring his love and truth to the people around us.

Also, I would be remiss not to tell you the impact of Karl's partnering efforts. Fayz gradually opened up to the gospel. He read the book we gave him. He asked Karl, Barbara, and their friends questions. But finally, almost a year after our initial ice cream shop interactions, Fayz, his wife, and their six-year-old daughter attended a Sunday morning service at Karl and Barbara's church. They walked in as devout adherents of Islam—but walked out an hour later as forgiven followers of their Savior and King, Jesus Christ.

Fayz's introduction to Jesus was a team effort: a variety of Christians with very different personalities and approaches, all cooperating with each other and with the Holy Spirit to reach a Muslim man and his family who are deeply loved by God.

These stories are just a glimpse of what's possible when you partner with fellow believers who have different outreach styles in order to influence your respective friends and family members in ways that fit each of them. So, seek out whatever approaches you need to supplement your own, knowing as the Bible tells us, "Two are better than one, because they have a good return for their labor" (Ecclesiastes 4:9). And, I might add, a whole team is usually better than two!

Sometimes We Need to Stretch

There will be occasions when God's assignment will be for you to stretch beyond your normal approach and be ready "in season and out of season" (2 Timothy 4:2) to do whatever it takes to share your faith with someone. I found myself in this position early in my walk with Christ, when my great uncle Maurice visited.

I hadn't seen him in years—and I knew I'd probably never see him again. He was getting up in age and suffering from a serious illness. Everyone in the family was aware that he was nearing the end of his life, which made his upcoming visit all the more poignant—and important. Everyone was also aware that Uncle Maurice's spiritual condition was at best unclear, though they didn't say it out loud.

When he finally arrived, Maurice was his usual good-natured self. Our family enjoyed the time with him, sharing meals and talking by the fireplace. In the midst of these pleasant conversations, though, I had a gnawing sense that God was leading me to talk with Maurice about the importance of knowing and following Christ while he still had the opportunity to do so. But I kept putting it off. After all, he was more than fifty years my senior.

Surely someone else in the family would be better equipped to talk with him!

More than that, describing it in the newer terms of the *Contagious Faith Styles*, I sensed that what Maurice needed was a direct, *Truth-Telling*-style challenge, and I recognized, even at that early stage of my development, that I tended to shy away from spiritual confrontation. If I'd known Karl at the time, I'm sure I would have tried to conscript *him* into the conversation. But I was on my own. God had chosen me for the moment, and I'd just have to stretch out of my comfort zone and let him use me in ways that felt foreign to me.

Finally, when I couldn't put it off any longer, I sat down on the chair across from Maurice, took a deep breath, and told him of my spiritual concerns for him. He smiled and gently told me I didn't need to worry about him. He was confident, he assured me, that God was kind and loving, and that he would be okay when the day came for him to pass on. "I've lived a pretty good life," he explained, "and I think God will see that and be fair to me."

"But that's not how it works," I responded emphatically, surprising even myself. Then I briefly walked him through the concept of sin and forgiveness, citing Romans 3:23.

Again, he tried to brush off my concerns, assuring me that he would be all right and that I had nothing to fear.

I realized it was *now or never*. A kind of holy boldness came over me. I slid from my chair onto the ottoman between us. Sitting directly in front of him, I gently grabbed both of his hands and looked straight into his eyes.

"Uncle Maurice," I said, "I love you enough to tell you the truth. It's only a matter of weeks or months or, at the very most, a few short years before you'll be standing in front of Jesus, and he is going to ask you whether you trusted in him and accepted his payment for your sins—so please don't turn away from him and his offer of eternal life!"

Maurice shrugged and thanked me for caring so deeply. He seemed touched by my love and concern, but he showed no signs of spiritual softening. A few days later he left. I followed up our conversation with a letter in which I again expressed my concerns and reminded him of his need to trust in Christ.

I never received a reply. Not long after that, we found out that Maurice had died.

I'll never know this side of eternity how he ultimately responded to my challenge. But I sensed the Holy Spirit's quiet affirmation, assuring me that my efforts had honored and pleased God. I've always been thankful that I trusted him and let him stretch me to challenge my great uncle. I was uncomfortable, but I had nothing to lose while Maurice had everything to gain.

Sharing our faith can be exciting and adventurous, but it's also *serious*. We're not merely trying to help people improve their lives. We're pointing them to Jesus, who unambiguously declared: "I am the way and the truth and the life. No one comes to the Father except through me" (John 14:6). We need to cultivate the courage to stretch occasionally beyond our natural approach in order to share him with the people we love, knowing that God is with us, and resting assured that our "labor in the Lord is not in vain" (1 Corinthians 15:58).

Always Rely on the Holy Spirit

Whether you are sharing your faith in partnership with other believers or on your own, and whether you're doing so in a way that fits you or one that feels like a real stretch, you can *always* count on the presence, power, and partnership of God's Spirit.

After Jesus commissioned us to "go and make disciples," he quickly added the promise, "and surely I am with you always, to the very end of the age" (Matthew 28:19–20). How is he with us? Through the Holy Spirit.

Jesus explained, "I will ask the Father, and he will give you another advocate to help you and be with you forever—the Spirit of truth. The world cannot accept him, because it neither sees him nor knows him. But you know him, for he lives with you and will be in you" (John 14:16–17). The Holy Spirit indwells all of us who are true followers of Christ (see Romans 8:9), and he is available to lead and empower us—especially when we're sharing the gospel with others.

I have seen and experienced this in many ways, but one of the most poignant examples of God's guidance comes from my friend Becky Pippert. An evangelistic legend, she wrote one of the all-time classic books on the topic, *Out of the Saltshaker and Into the World*. In her more recent book, *Stay Salt*, she tells a story that shows the power available to us when we seek the Holy Spirit's help and guidance in reaching people for him.

During a time when Becky and her husband were living in Ireland, Becky was determined to talk about her faith with her manicurist, Heather, before flying home to Michigan the next day. They'd known each other for two years, during which it became clear to Becky that Heather was more interested in fashion and beauty than she was in God. On the way to the salon, she prayed, "Lord, I have tried everything to rouse Heather's curiosity in the gospel. But she just isn't interested. If there is a way to reach her, then you, Lord, will have to do it, because I cannot."

When Becky walked into the salon, she started to grab a magazine from the top of a pile like she normally would, but she suddenly felt the urge to take a magazine from the middle of the stack. "It was almost as if there was a big arrow pointing to it!" she reports.

Then she went to Heather's table for her manicure. She was flipping through the magazine when she realized that she knew one of the models staring back at her from the pages. That caught Heather's attention. She was impressed that Becky knew a model in *Vogue*. Then Becky remembered that the model, Jenny, had gone through a spiritual search that had changed her life in dramatic ways. She suddenly recognized this as the opportunity she had prayed for.

In that instant I realized what God had done. Fashion and beauty were Heather's "mother ship." To hear anything about the life of a fashion model fascinated her. So I told her about Jenny's search for meaning, what drew her to Christ, and why the gospel had made so much sense to her.

Heather listened in rapt attention. Then she asked me if I had any books on the Christian faith that she could read. Before we left for the airport the next morning, I dropped off some books that were written for seekers.

What does this story tell us? The Lord of the universe, the Maker of heaven and earth, passionately longs for his creation to know him—and that includes a 21-year-old nail technician whose primary interest is fashion. I had walked into the shop saying to the Lord, "I can't reach her, so you must." It was almost as if the Lord was saying, *Step aside, Becky; I will show you how it's done!* . . .

In his grace and mercy God desires that we collaborate with him in reaching people with the good news of Jesus. His Spirit can nudge us to pick out just the right magazine, because he knows that that magazine will be the very catalyst that will enable us to share the gospel with that particular person. Is there anything more exciting than being in the hands of the living God?!

. . . Here's the truth we must learn by heart: God uses the weak to reveal his glory! Yes, we are inadequate, but we are also in partnership with the living God! And that changes everything . . .[1]

Partnering with the Living God

Earlier I discussed ways we can work to reach people in partnership with each other, but I also love what Becky said about us working "in partnership with the living God!" It echoes what Paul said in 1 Corinthians 3:6–7, "I planted the seed, Apollos watered it, but *God has been making it grow. So neither the one who plants nor the one who waters is anything, but only God, who makes things grow*" (emphasis mine).

Spreading the gospel is ultimately *God's* business—and we have the privilege of joining him in what *he* is doing to reach our world. More than that, we need to pray the way Becky did, asking him to work in and through us, to open up opportunities, and then to give us the courage to seize them. Yes, prayer and partnering with the Holy Spirit are indispensable aspects of helping build God's kingdom in our individual corners of the world.

If we're ever tempted to think we can go it alone, reaching people through our own strength and wisdom without God's power working through us and in the other person, then we need to go back to Scripture and remind ourselves how deep the sin condition really is.

Romans 3:10–12 explains:

> There is no one righteous, not even one;
>> there is no one who understands;
>> there is no one who seeks God.
> All have turned away,
>> they have together become worthless;
> there is no one who does good,
>> not even one.

That's a sobering but honest assessment of the human condition. Thankfully Jesus told his disciples, "Very truly I tell you, it is for your good that I am going away. Unless I go away, the Advocate will not come to you; but if I go, I will send him to you. When he comes, *he will prove the world to be in the wrong about sin and righteousness and judgment*" (John 16:7–8, emphasis mine). It's that Advocate, the Holy Spirit, who works in the hearts of sinful people—people who don't naturally or independently want to know God—and enables them to ask, to seek, and to knock until they finally find Christ (Matthew 7:7–8).

Here are some ways we can intentionally rely upon the Holy Spirit:

- Pray, pray, and keep praying for your lost friends, relatives, and neighbors. Ask God to open their spiritual eyes and to *prove them in the wrong about sin and righteousness and judgment*. A convicting question has been making the rounds on social media over the last couple of years. It asks, "If today God saved everyone whose salvation you prayed for yesterday, would there be any new people in his kingdom?" I don't know about you, but I have to remind myself frequently to keep on praying for people who don't yet know him. Nothing could be more important.

- Ask God to increase your wisdom, knowledge, and sensitivity to his leadings. Ask him for chances to share your faith, along with the eyes to see those opportunities and the courage to seize them.

- Pray for the Holy Spirit's power to be working and evident in the other person's life. Ask him to reveal himself to them in ways that open doors and overcome intellectual and spiritual barriers. Ask him to use you to help "demolish arguments and every pretension that sets itself up against the knowledge of God," in order to "take captive every thought to make it obedient to Christ" (2 Corinthians 10:5).

- Jesus said to "Ask the Lord of the harvest, therefore, to send out workers into his harvest field" (Luke 10:2). Pray specifically for "workers" who can become effective partners with you in reaching out to your friends and acquaintances, even as you partner with them to reach theirs.

- Together with like-minded believers, pray for the salvation of the people in all your lives who need to find and follow Christ—including (or perhaps, *especially*) those you view as unlikely candidates for the gospel. Pray that God will use you to help fulfill Jesus's mission "to seek and save the lost" (Luke 19:10).

- Ask God to guide you to plant spiritual seeds in "good soil," and to produce a spiritual crop that is "a hundred times what was sown" (Matthew 13:1–23). What would that look like, exactly? I don't know, but by God's Spirit it can become "immeasurably more than all we ask or imagine, according to his power that is at work within us" (Ephesians 3:20).

I hope you're seeing that living out a contagious faith is nothing less than an exhilarating and rewarding adventure. If we'll intentionally partner with other like-minded believers who have different styles than we do, if we'll stretch to tell people about Christ even when it's not a perfect fit for our natural style, and if we'll rely on the Holy Spirit to work in and through us and to make us partners of God in this grand redemptive mission, then there's no telling what might happen.

This is especially true when we add in one other element that is often missing from our lives. What element? We'll explore *that* question next!

CHAPTER 10

EXPERIENCING THE
UNEXPECTED ADVENTURE

For God has not given us a spirit of fear and
timidity, but of power, love, and self-discipline. So
never be ashamed to tell others about our Lord.

—2 TIMOTHY 1:7-8 NLT

I bought my first serious mountain bike when I was living in Southern California—a full-suspension, carbon-fiber, high-performance trail beast with all the latest tech and features—and riding off-road there was a real *adventure.*

You might be thinking, *Southern California—isn't that the land of seashores, sandy beaches, and endless summers? How adventurous could it be?*

Well, I wasn't tooling around a church parking lot or pedaling down the boardwalks of a seaside village. I lived in the foothills of the Santa Ana Mountains where the trails can be intense. I realized this while riding down a hill near my home. The pitch was so steep that when I tried to slow down, I ended up flipping forward, head-over-heels, ending up flat on my back with my upside-down bike suspended in the air directly above me.

Welcome to the world of real mountain biking, I muttered under my breath, as I dusted off my shoulders (and ego) and got back in the saddle. That was my first tumble—but definitely not my last.

Mountain biking in that area wasn't the safest pastime. Besides the treacherous inclines, sandy slopes, washed-out trails, big boulders, and sliding rocks, as well as sudden turns next to sheer cliffs, there were also bobcats, coyotes, and the occasional rattlesnake. Not to mention the mountain lions—which can weigh up to two hundred pounds and sprint as fast as fifty miles an hour. And since that time, I've moved to the Colorado Rockies, where we have most of those same dangers as well as very large black bears!

And you know what? Those very elements make my bike outings much more exhilarating. What started as mere exercise has become an exciting adventure.

Here's what I've realized: adventure always involves at least some measure of the unexpected. In fact, Merriam-Webster's definition for the word *adventure* is "an undertaking usually involving danger and unknown risk."[1]

What's true about outdoor adventure is also true of spiritual adventure. Real excitement requires some *risk*—and that's the missing element in many of our lives as Christians.

Bored Believers

"The word 'Christian' means different things to different people," explains Eugene Peterson in his book *Traveling Light* (IVP). "To one person it means a stiff, upright, inflexible way of life, colorless and unbending. To another, it means a risky, surprise-filled venture, lived tiptoe at the edge of expectation . . ." And, Peterson adds, "If we get our information from the biblical material, there is no doubt that the Christian life is a dancing, leaping, daring life."[2]

Truth be told, many of us try to live faithful Christian lives, but we're not experiencing anything close to a "surprise-filled venture, lived tiptoe at the edge of expectation." Instead, we easily slip into a predictable, routine, and sometimes mechanical religious existence.

In a word, many of us are spiritually *bored*. Why is that? It's because we aren't taking risks, trying new things, or going out on a limb of faith where we're furthering God's purposes while relying on him to come through to help us. Our spiritual lives are not adventurous because there's little at stake in how we're living them.

And what more rewarding way to take risks than in reaching out to others with the greatest news on the planet?

"I've never heard a Christian say they're feeling spiritually dry, and then in the next breath talk about all the people they're trying to reach for Christ," said a pastor friend. "The two just don't go together. If you're actively involved in sharing the gospel, then you're going to feel spiritually alive. You'll feel reliant on God's guidance and power, and that will draw you closer to him. But if you're not reaching out to others—well, then your Christian life can quickly become parched and predictable."

Increasing your involvement in outreach injects adrenaline into every other aspect of your Christian life. Suddenly you find yourself praying more fervently because you're lifting up your friends who don't know God, asking for his intervention and salvation. You're studying the Bible more thoroughly because you know you might get asked questions about your faith. Your worship becomes deeper because you're exalting the God who doesn't just love us but also so loves people all around the world for whom "he gave his one and only Son, that *whoever* believes in him shall not perish but have eternal life" (John 3:16, emphasis mine).

"The joy of the LORD is your strength," says Nehemiah (in Nehemiah 8:10). Just wait until you see how your joy and strength are bolstered when one of your friends puts their trust in Christ after you've taken a risk to share the message of Jesus with them. Your faith will be *electrified*! You'll suddenly find yourself running around like King David, declaring "I can run through a troop and leap over a wall!" (see Psalm 18:29).

Regardless of which *Contagious Faith Style* is yours, a little evangelistic risk a day will definitely help keep the spiritual boredom away!

The Courage to Take Risks

This topic of spiritual risk-taking seems exciting, but let's be honest: we'll need to muster a bit of courage to begin moving into greater degrees of God-honoring risk. And this is true no matter who you are or how long you've been involved in sharing your faith.

I was teaching at a conference where I had some time to chat with a friend who had shared his faith since he was a very young man. "I'm curious," I said. "After all this time, do you ever still get nervous before talking to someone about Christ?"

Without hesitating, he replied: "Yes, of course—always!"

I can't tell you how encouraging that was to me. Why? Because that man was the renowned evangelist Luis Palau. He reached people for *six decades*, spoke in *seventy-five countries*, and presented the gospel to *a billion people*.[3] And he was a ministry hero of mine.

Breaking the ice spiritually isn't easy for anyone. Yet here was a man who'd been overcoming his inherent nervousness year after year in countless settings around the world, and finding that each time he did so, God showed up to help him spiritually influence the people he spoke to.

Thankfully, we have a rich heritage of evangelistic courage in the Christian church. Think of the blind man Jesus healed in John 9—our example of the *Story-Sharing* style. Within minutes of receiving his sight he singlehandedly took on the religious hierarchy that was already conspiring to get rid of Jesus. They brought the man in for questioning, and in the process of interacting with him they admitted they didn't even know where Jesus came from. "Now that is remarkable!" he responded. "You don't know where he comes from, yet he opened my eyes . . . Nobody has ever heard of opening the eyes of a man born blind. If this man were not from God, he could do nothing" (verses 30–33). His courage got him expelled from that gathering, but the risks he took to speak for Jesus have inspired millions over the past two millennia.

Consider the bravery of Ananias in Damascus who, according to Acts 9:10–15, was led by God to go and pray for Saul, the persecutor of the church who had overseen the stoning of Stephen. God wanted Ananias to restore Saul's sight, which he'd lost when he saw the risen Jesus on the Road to Damascus. "Lord," Ananias answered, "I have heard many reports about this man and all the harm he has done to your holy people in Jerusalem. And he has come here with authority from the chief priests to arrest all who call on your name" (verses 13–14). But God said to Ananias: "Go! This man is my chosen instrument to proclaim my name to the Gentiles and their kings and to the people of Israel" (verse 15)—and Ananias went! It felt like an enormous risk, but he'll forever be remembered as the servant of God who courageously helped the persecutor Saul be transformed into the apostle Paul.

And remember Paul himself, our *Reason-Giving* exemplar who took the risk of challenging the academic intelligentsia of Athens. He debated spiritual truth with them and, as we've seen, he was able to not only stand his ground but with God's help he won some of them over to become followers of Christ. Paul took countless risks as he traversed the world declaring the gospel. And it was Paul who admonished Timothy—and through him, every one of us—"For God has not given us a spirit of fear and timidity, but of power, love, and self-discipline. So never be ashamed to tell others about our Lord" (2 Timothy 1:7–8 NLT).

Also, here's an example from former journalist Lee Strobel's life, soon after he left behind his skepticism to become a Christian. It's easy to forget that well-known apologists like Lee, just like you and me, had to start at the awkward beginning stage. In fact, he shares a story about one of his early ventures into evangelism that took some courage—and which didn't seem to go well, at least initially. Here's his account of what happened.

> One average and routine day I was packing up my briefcase and getting ready to leave the newspaper when I felt a gentle nudging of the Holy Spirit. I sensed God wanted me to go into the business office and invite my friend, who was an atheist, to come to Easter services at my church. Since the impression seemed so strong, I figured something dramatic was going to happen. And it did—but not in the way I had anticipated.

I walked into the business office and looked around. The place appeared empty except for my friend, who was sitting at his desk. *Perfect!* I reminded him that Easter was coming and asked if he would want to come to our church with Leslie and me. He turned me down cold. I asked if he was interested at all in spiritual matters, and he emphatically said no. I asked if he had any questions about God, and again he said no. I talked to him about why the resurrection was so important, but he clearly wasn't interested.

With all of my evangelistic overtures being instantly shut down, I was beginning to get a little embarrassed. Why was he so disinterested in talking about spiritual matters if God was indeed prodding me to talk with him? Finally, I stammered, "Well, uh, if you've ever got any questions, um, I guess you know where my desk is," and I walked out.

What was that all about? I couldn't understand why he was so adamantly resistant. In the end, I concluded that maybe I was going to be one link in a very long chain of people and experiences that would eventually lead him to Christ. Still, as far as I know he remains a skeptic to this day.

Fast-forward several years. By this time I was a teaching pastor at a church in suburban Chicago. After I spoke one Sunday morning, a middle-aged man came up, shook my hand, and said, "I just want to thank you for the spiritual influence you've had in my life."

"That's very nice," I said. "But who are you?"

"Let me tell you my story," he replied. "A few years ago I lost my job. I didn't have any money and I was afraid I was going to lose my house. I called a friend of mine who runs a newspaper and said, 'Do you have any work for me?' He asked,

'Can you tile floors?' Well, I had tiled my bathroom once, so I said, 'Sure.' He told me, 'We need some tiling done at the newspaper; if you can do that, we can pay you.'

"So one day, not long before Easter, I was on my hands and knees behind a desk in the business office of the newspaper, fixing some tiles, when you walked into the room. I don't think you even saw me. You started talking about God and Jesus and Easter and the church to some guy, and he wasn't interested at all. But I was crouching there listening, and my heart was beating fast, and I started thinking, *I need God! I need to go to church!*

"As soon as you left, I called my wife and said, 'We're going to church this Easter.' She said, 'You're kidding!' I said, 'No, we are.' We ended up going to your church that Easter—and my wife, my teenage son, and I all came to faith in Christ. And I just wanted to thank you!"

I was dumbstruck! Who could have foreseen that, except the amazing God of grace?[4]

Lee's story underscores how mustering up a little courage to take even a small spiritual risk—as he did when he walked into that office to talk to his colleague about Christ—can be used by God to produce huge results. It also helps you understand why we call such experiences *unexpected adventures!*

Split-Second Spiritual Decisions

Often we face moments when we ask ourselves, *Should I or shouldn't I?* How we answer the question will determine whether or not we'll have a lasting spiritual influence on the people around us.

Should I or shouldn't I? That was the decision I was pondering after our waiter, leaning against a pillar near our table in a popular pizza parlor, gave us the open-ended invitation, "Just let me know if you have any questions."

Heidi and I had recently moved to Chicago so I could attend graduate school. As I began to work on my master's degree in philosophy of religion, my mind was filled with lofty ideas along with lists of challenging assignments—so it was a relief for us to get away for dinner with another couple we'd befriended at the university.

I'm sure the waiter was expecting us to ask a question about, say, which of the establishment's founding family members came up with their secret recipes or what was so special about their deep-dish crust. But I was struck by the open-endedness of his offer: "Let me know if you have any questions."

I've got lots of questions, I thought. *Maybe I'll have some fun and put what I've been reading from Immanuel Kant to good use. Perhaps God could use it to get us talking about things that really matter. Should I go for it?*

We make these kinds of decisions almost daily. We routinely encounter opportunities in which we ask ourselves—consciously or subconsciously—*Should I or shouldn't I?*

It's at this precise juncture that we decide whether to take the courageous way *into* the conversation, or the seemingly safer way *out* of it. Unfortunately, many of us are so accustomed to taking the escape route that we barely realize there was an opportunity or decision in front of us at all. But being willing to take God-guided risks at these conversational intersections is what will determine whether or not we'll have a truly contagious faith.

I haven't always taken the courageous route in, but thankfully I did that time.

"Yes," I replied to the waiter. "I have a really important question. I've been reading Immanuel Kant's book *Critique of Pure Reason* for one of my grad school classes, and I was wondering: Do you think that the categories of the mind apply to the noumenal world in the same way they apply to the phenomenal world?"

He looked at me quizzically, a bit startled. Then he broke into a smile and playfully shot back, "I'm not sure—but I once heard about a scientist who looked through his telescope and thought he saw *God!* Pretty strange, huh?"

"That's not at all strange," I said, determined to keep the conversation flowing. "I don't know if this was the guy you heard about, but I recently read an interesting book by a well-known scientist named Robert Jastrow, called *God and the Astronomers.* It was his observation of the incredible order and intricacy of the universe that led him to finally conclude that there must be a God. And his book shook up a lot of people in the scientific community."

"Wow, that's interesting," he replied. "I don't really think about God too much. What did you say the name of that book was?"

And just like that, we were off and running with a serious spiritual conversation. Suddenly we were discussing the scientific evidence that supports biblical belief, followed by some of us at our table briefly describing the difference that knowing Christ makes in our lives.

We eventually got around to ordering our pizza, but I don't remember much about the food that evening. What stands out in my mind was that we engaged in a short but stimulating conversation, during which we had the opportunity to talk about Jesus with this young man—and how it stemmed from what seemed at the time like an eccentric impulse to throw out an offbeat remark.

And it didn't end there. Because of our waiter's interest in science and faith, I asked if he'd like to read the book I'd mentioned, and he said he would. So, a few days later I brought him my copy, along with a few other resources I thought would be helpful in his spiritual journey.

I never had another opportunity to interact with him, but I was glad I took a small risk that evening by tossing out an unusual question. As a result, the four of us had the chance to tell someone about Jesus.

Only God knows how our efforts might be used in that man's life over the long haul. And either way, it turned what would otherwise have been an ordinary culinary outing into an unexpected evangelistic adventure. Just telling this story again makes me want to take more risks for the sake of people like him, who need to know the love and forgiveness of the Savior. (Oh, and yes, to get some more deep-dish pizza!)

I hope it has the same impact on you (the evangelism part, not necessarily the pizza part), and that with God's help you too will start stepping up more often to seize these kinds of exhilarating outreach opportunities. There's simply no telling what the spiritual ripple effects might be.

Launching into Unexpected Adventures

Your most significant evangelistic encounters will often come out of unexpected junctures like the one I just described, after you make a courageous split-second decision to bring up spiritual matters. You might not be thinking about such things in the moment or be aware of the opportunity that's about to present itself. But suddenly you'll see it and think to yourself: *Should I or shouldn't I? I'm not really "prayed up," I don't know what I would say next if the person shows interest, and I'm certainly not ready to answer a lot of deep theological questions.*

My advice? Ignore all that internal noise and jump into the opportunity anyway. God can guide and use you, but first you must take the small risk of getting the conversation going!

That said, I'm all for getting ready ahead of time, and doing so will only increase your confidence when opportunities arise. Peter told us to "be prepared to give an answer" (1 Peter 3:15). You've taken a good first step by reading this book. A natural next step is to pursue training that will help you hone some of the skills we've discussed in these pages. I'd urge you to rally your small group, class, or entire congregation to go through our six-week *Contagious Faith* video training course.[5] I'll come to your gathering via video and help every member discover their style of evangelism and "be prepared" in this vital area. And by doing this together you'll discover each other's styles, as well as how you can intentionally partner to reach family and friends. Information on the course can be found on the *Recommended Resources* section, where you'll also find details about our university courses and certificates available in these areas through the Lee Strobel Center for Evangelism and Applied Apologetics.

Another way you can be prepared for these unexpected opportunities is to carry evangelistic books and materials with you that you can use as "spiritual backup." As you've probably noticed, one of my frequent next steps when I have spiritual conversations is to give the person a book, Bible, DVD, or similar resource. Having a supply of such ministry tools will increase your confidence in bringing up spiritual matters, and they can extend your influence after you're gone. I've listed a few of my favorite give-away resources on the *Recommended Resources* page as well. I'd urge you to have materials like these ready in your computer case, backpack, purse, glove compartment, and desk drawer. It's a small investment that can yield rich rewards.

Regardless of the approach you take or what resources you use, remember that ultimately we need to share the central message of the gospel—the story of King Jesus and his redemptive work on our behalf—as well as details on how the person can receive his forgiveness and leadership. I'll say it once more: our goal is not to simply have spiritual discussions or to win theological debates; it's to win people to Jesus Christ.

Be willing to take small spiritual risks—then bigger ones as your confidence grows. This is essential to finding excitement and adventure in your spiritual life, and it's often the turning point in the journey of the people you're seeking to reach. The key is to make courageous split-second decisions and intentionally move *into* spiritual conversations. And I have a simple but helpful plan for doing just that.

Ready? Whenever you sense that God is providing an opportunity to talk to someone about him, do the following four things:

Take a deep breath, say a quick prayer, open your mouth, and *blurt it out!*

- *Take a deep breath:* Funny thing, but outreach always goes best when you have plenty of oxygen in your lungs.
- *Say a quick prayer:* Ask God to lead and use you. But it must be brief—about the amount of time required to take the deep breath.

- *Open your mouth:* This makes your words much easier to understand.
- *Blurt it out:* You've got air in your lungs, God on your side, and an important message to share; what more could you possibly want? Speak up and spark some spiritual action. Don't delay, don't change the subject, and don't give the devil time to whisper in your ear that this is not an opportune moment. Just launch into the adventure and watch God work!

God will honor your efforts! He will use you in ways you can't even imagine. And if you'll do these things consistently over time, you'll end up leaving a spiritual legacy that impacts both heaven and earth.

CHAPTER 11

LEAVING A LASTING LEGACY

I consider my life worth nothing to me; my
only aim is to finish the race and complete the
task the Lord Jesus has given me—the task of
testifying to the good news of God's grace.

—APOSTLE PAUL IN ACTS 20:24

"I have HAD it! I'm going to get as far away from here as I possibly can!"

Orland was still a teenager, but he was fed up with the pressures of living under the same roof as an alcoholic father who was angry and often emotionally abusive.

How badly did he want to escape his stressful home? Enough to enlist in the Navy in early 1945, despite World War II still raging—and with the main front of the fighting shifting to the naval battles in the Pacific. Undaunted, Orland signed the papers, announced his departure, and at age seventeen—the youngest age the Navy allowed—he headed off to basic training in Illinois.

But then while he was in the middle of boot camp, the war suddenly ended. So instead of going out to fight, he was assigned to a peacetime post at Millington Naval Base, just a few miles outside of Memphis, Tennessee.

After a season of serving there, Orland met his new boss, Chief Petty Officer Bill Abraham. He soon discovered that Abraham was both a straight shooter and a committed believer. Not long after getting acquainted, in fact, Abraham looked Orland in the eye and asked him if he was a Christian. He answered in the affirmative, assuring him that, "I'm a church member, I was confirmed, I've read the Bible, and I have prayed."

In the classic *Truth-Telling* style, Abraham responded by asking Orland pointedly, "How do those things make you a Christian?"

This led to stimulating spiritual discussions, and in the *Friendship-Building* style, Abraham soon formed a real relationship with Orland—or "Ollie," as he called him. The more they talked, the more Orland realized that he was relying on his church background and good deeds to make him right with God, rather than the work of Christ on his behalf. This truth became clearer and clearer the more they talked, and especially when Abraham began taking him to a Bible study with some of his friends.

Orland was drawn to the people he was meeting and the message he was hearing, but he was still resistant. He fit Paul's description of people who "act religious" yet "reject the power that could make them godly" (2 Timothy 3:5 NLT). Perhaps it was the residual effects of his rocky relationship with his father, but it wasn't easy for him to simply trust in Christ. What would it take to get through to this young man?

One day, Abraham heard about a series of revival meetings coming to their area. Sponsored by an upstart ministry called Youth for Christ, these events were to be held in the large Ellis Auditorium in downtown Memphis. The featured speaker would be a well-known radio personality and evangelist named Charles E. Fuller. So, Abraham urged his young friend to get a bus ticket, head to Memphis, and attend a night of the revival.

Orland was hesitant. He sent off a letter to the one other committed Christian he knew—his mother, Effa, back in Lincoln, Nebraska. He remembered that she often listened to Fuller's Old Fashioned Revival Hour on Sunday afternoons. Orland told her about the event and Fuller's involvement. "Do you think I should go?" he asked.

Effa, of course, saw this as a divine answer to her fervent prayers. "Yes, son," she wrote back immediately. "I would certainly encourage you to attend!" So, Orland made his way to Memphis for what promised to be an interesting evening. The date was October 9, 1946.

When the night came, Orland, wearing his Navy whites, sat alone in the upper side balcony—close to a door so he could escape if necessary. But as the program unfolded, he found himself strangely warming to the music and then to the message from Dr. Fuller.

Finally, at the end of the sermon, the choir director led the auditorium full of people in singing, "Just As I Am."

> *Just as I am, without one plea*
> *But that Thy blood was shed for me*
> *And that Thou bid'st me come to Thee*
> *O Lamb of God, I come! I come!*

Fuller stood at the podium again and said he wanted to pray for anyone who was willing to respond, "without one plea" and receive Jesus into their life. He asked anyone who would like to do this to quietly raise their hand. As for Orland, he lifted his hand high! Fuller looked up to the balcony, pointed at him, and jubilantly exclaimed, "I see your hand, young sailor boy—God bless ya!"

Orland didn't know what was going to happen next, but when an usher asked him if he'd like to come pray with someone to make Jesus his Savior, it was like he had a spring in his seat. He jumped out of his chair, bolted down the stairs, and made his way to the front of the auditorium where Dr. Fuller was on the stage. Fuller led everyone who responded to the invitation in a prayer to receive Christ as their Savior, including Orland. He prayed along sincerely and immediately felt a sense of relief, knowing his sins had been forgiven and his life was now under new management.

Orland never looked back. Under the mentorship of Abraham, he grew quickly in his understanding of the faith and in his relationship with Christ. During his first visit home, the eldest of his four younger sisters, Martie, asked what had happened to him. Using his own *Story-Sharing* style, he unfolded the details of his spiritual journey to her. She was intrigued, and they ended up kneeling and praying together as she received Jesus as *her* forgiver and leader. Before long, all of his siblings received Christ and eventually, he believes, his recovering alcoholic father did as well.

With Abraham's encouragement, Orland left the Navy to enroll at Wheaton College in Wheaton, Illinois. That's where he met a number of great new friends—including Billy Graham's sister, Jeanie, and the man she would marry, evangelist Leighton Ford. He also got to know Jim Elliot and Nate Saint—two outstanding young Christians who, along with three other friends, would shock the world a few years later when they were martyred as missionaries in Ecuador (a story later told in the classic, *Through the Gates of Splendor*, by Elisabeth Elliot, as well as the more recent book and movie, *End of the Spear*). Orland's experience at Wheaton inspired him to serve Christ wholeheartedly through his chosen field of business management.

As he neared graduation in 1951, he met a Christian nursing student named Virginia at a fellowship group that was part of College Church in Wheaton. She caught his eye and then captured his heart, and the two were married about a year later. They chose a theme verse for their union: "O magnify the LORD with me, and let us exalt his name together" (Psalm 34:3 KJV).

Orland and Ginny served God while he built his career, and they committed to raising their four children "in the nurture and admonition of the Lord" (Ephesians 6:4 KJV). The couple impacted the lives of untold people in the various places they lived, in the churches where they volunteered, through having Orland share his testimony at various places, and they even helped start a Youth for Christ chapter—in honor of the ministry that helped reach him so many years earlier. Their lives and ministry together flourished for almost seven decades—until Ginny finally passed away in November of 2019.

Leaving a Spiritual Legacy

What's the point of this story, and how do I know so much about a post-World War II sailor? Well, *I was Orland and Ginny's third-born child!*

I grew up in the Christian faith and, in spite of my many spiritual ups and downs during the high school years, at age nineteen I finally stopped resisting God's guiding hand and, following in the footsteps of my godly parents, gave my life unreservedly to Jesus.

What's more, my two sisters, Lisa and Kathy, as well as my brother, Gary, are all following Christ along with their spouses today—as did all of my father's siblings. And, thankfully, many of my parents' grandkids and great grandkids are walking with Jesus too, and we're praying for those who aren't quite there yet. Also, Heidi's and my two kids, Emma Jean and Matthew, are following the Lord and serving him in ministry roles.

And what about Orland? As I write this, he is 94 years old and continues to have a spiritual influence among staff and other residents at the retirement community where he now lives. In fact, not long ago he helped lead his buddy Steven, a younger man from a nearby town, to faith in Christ. And today my father is one of my closest friends and confidants.

Do you see what emerged from the evangelistic efforts of our own "Father Abraham"? One day so many years ago, faced with a young naval recruit, Bill Abraham decided to take a spiritual risk. He asked himself, *Should I or shouldn't I?*—and then he simply *did*. He made a courageous split-second decision and asked Orland if he was a real Christian. This small step unleashed a spiritual chain reaction that has impacted innumerable lives and families through the decades. And the ripple effects continue to spread around the world.

Bill Abraham's legacy became Orland Mittelberg's legacy, and Orland's legacy became mine (and my family's). And if I can influence you to find your *Contagious Faith Style* and effectively reach out to others for Christ, then my legacy will become yours—and you'll want to pass it on to even more generations as well!

As Paul encouraged Timothy, I want to encourage you: "Be strong in the grace that is in Christ Jesus. And the things you have heard me say . . . entrust to reliable people who will also be qualified to teach others" (2 Timothy 2:1–2). That's the blueprint for how God is using us to change the world.

A Contagious Epidemic

My dad's story is just a small sliver of what God is doing around the globe. I recently read a book by my friends Michael Brown and Craig Keener in which they cite amazing statistics about what I believe is part of an evangelistic tipping point that's occurring in other parts of the world. As these examples show, we truly seem to be in at least the beginnings of a spiritually contagious international epidemic. I think you'll find these trends encouraging, especially in light of some of the sobering news we hear about the church here in the West.[1]

- The number of Christians in Indonesia has grown from 1.3 million forty years ago to over 11 million today. (*Operation World*)
- If Bible translation had continued at its historic pace, providing a Bible in every people group's heart language would have been accomplished in 2150. But thanks to God's working through *Wycliffe's Vision 2025*, the work has been accelerated by over 100 years and is now on pace to be completed in 2042. (*Wycliffe*)
- *The Jesus Film* has been translated into nearly 1,000 languages and over 200,000,000 people have indicated decisions for Christ as a result of the film. (*Campus Crusade*)

- No Christian was officially allowed to live in Nepal until 1960. Now there is a church in every one of the seventy-five districts of Nepal with estimates of over half a million believers. (*Operation World*)
- About 500 Muslims come to faith in Christ every month in Iran—a country ranked among the top ten persecutors of Christians in the world. Many of the new believers are young, since 70 percent of Iran is under the age of thirty. (*Vision 2020*)
- Every day, 20,000 Africans come to Christ. Africa was 3 percent Christian in 1900 and is now over 50 percent Christian. (*Vision 2020*)
- In 1900, Korea had no Protestant church and the country was deemed impossible to penetrate. Today South Korea is 30 percent Christian with 7,000 churches in Seoul alone, and several of these churches have over 1,000,000 members. (*Vision 2020*)
- There are currently 60–80 million Christians in China, with between 10,000 and 25,000 converts a day. (*Open Doors*)

Brown and Keener also add this encouraging information from a missionary organization called The Traveling Team:[2]

The number of people who are being presented the plan of salvation every day is now at least 260,274. . . . Every day now the average number added to the body of Christ worldwide averages 174,000. 3,500 new churches are opening every week worldwide. Our annual growth rate of church planting is presently at more than 8% per year. We only need 11% per annum to allow us to place a living Christian fellowship—a local church—as a witness in every community in the entire world. We have seen countries like Singapore have a 10% increase of those who have seen Christ come into their lives.

In the 1980s 10% of Korea and 10% of Chile turned to Christ, and over 10% in Indonesia—the largest Muslim country in the world. Indonesia is now over 25% Christian.

"Even if some of these statistics are too optimistic," Brown and Keener conclude, "they present a very different picture than one of a defeated and demoralized Church. This is not the failure of Christianity, this is the triumph of the Gospel, to the point that *in one day*, around the world, far more people come to faith in Jesus than may have come to faith in Him in the first seventy years of Church history. And this is exactly what we should expect, since Revelation 7 speaks of 'a great multitude that no one could number, from every nation, from all tribes and peoples and languages'" (Revelation 7:9).[3]

As we stretch to share the Good News with the people around us, we're participating in a growing worldwide movement through which God is bringing his salvation to the ends of the earth. We're seeing the tangible fulfillment of the promise of Jesus that, "I will build my church, and the gates of hell shall not prevail against it" (Matthew 16:18 ESV).

Eternal Investments

Let's face it: There aren't many things you can do in this world that really last. Most of the things we give so much of our time and energy to die out even before we do. And the ones that outlive us usually endure, at most, for a generation or two—and then our efforts are forgotten.

"Everything is meaningless . . ." said Solomon, the writer of Ecclesiastes. "No one remembers the former generations, and even those yet to come will not be remembered by those who follow them" (Ecclesiastes 1:2, 11).

Well, that may be true in ordinary human terms. But in God's greater world, things have a lot longer shelf life—that is, an *eternal* one! It's worth letting this sink in: The only things that last forever besides God and his heavenly kingdom are *people*.

No, we can't take any of our possessions, accomplishments, or trophies with us. But we can take our family members. Our sons and daughters. Our grandkids. Our parents. Our siblings. Our aunts and uncles. Our cousins. Our friends. Our coworkers. Our neighbors. Even the guy who fixes our car, or the folks who dry-clean our clothes.

Every one of them was created in the image of God, and they were made to know him. But they need to be reached. They need to hear the Good News, and perhaps the story of how God reached and redeemed you. They need spiritual answers and some assistance in putting the puzzle pieces together.

Working with the Holy Spirit as well as other believers with different styles from your own, you can help them see the big picture. You can help them understand that they are morally bankrupt but still highly valued. In fact, the sinless Son of God left behind the perks of heaven and laid down his life to pay for their sins. Then he rose from the dead to prove that it was all true and to offer them new life.

And he commissions us to be his representatives, telling our friends and loved ones—as well as people we meet along the road of life—that the God of the universe cares about *them* and wants to redeem them, adopt them into his family, reach others through them, and ultimately usher them into heaven with him and with each other. Now that's Good News we ought to get excited about sharing whenever we can!

Because when we do, God will be with us—guiding our words and empowering our actions. He'll use us—no, he'll use *you*—to impact the lives of the people around you in ways that will last for all of eternity. Who knows what spiritual chain reactions your efforts might trigger? The ripple effects are destined to go down through the generations.

Nothing—absolutely nothing—could be more important than discovering and using your unique faith-sharing style in order to lead people to the Savior and then to equip them to do the same. It's the primary purpose for which God left us on this planet! And in the end, the family members and friends you reach will thank you, God will bless and reward you, and you'll feel an unending sense of gratitude, knowing he used you to impact lives, both now and forever.

So, lift up your eyes. Expand your vision. God is building his kingdom, and the King is calling you to get on the frontlines of the effort. Trust that he can use you. Find your style, work to develop it, and take risks to put it into play. One thing's for sure: He will use you in ways you can't yet fathom.

"Now to him who is able to do immeasurably more than all we ask or imagine, according to his power that is at work within us, to him be glory in the church and in Christ Jesus throughout all generations, for ever and ever! Amen" (Ephesians 3:20–21).

RECOMMENDED RESOURCES

Training Courses on Sharing Your Faith

Contagious Faith Training Course: Discover Your Natural Style for Sharing Jesus with Others, Mark Mittelberg, Zondervan, 2021 (this 6-week video course will help you and the members of your small group, class, youth ministry, or entire church learn your natural evangelism styles and begin to master the Key Skills discussed in the *Contagious Faith* book).

Making Your Case for Christ: An Action Plan for Sharing What You Believe and Why, Lee Strobel and Mark Mittelberg, Zondervan, 2018 (this 6-week video course trains participants in elements of both apologetics and personal evangelism).

Certificate courses on innovative evangelism and practical apologetics are available online through Colorado Christian University. Accredited bachelor's and master's degrees may also be earned online. See: StrobelCenter.com.

Other Books on Sharing Your Faith

The Unexpected Adventure: Taking Everyday Risks to Talk with People about Jesus, Lee Strobel and Mark Mittelberg, Zondervan, 2009 (draws from the authors' real-life stories to inspire and encourage readers in sharing Christ with others).

How to Talk About Jesus (Without Being THAT Guy): Personal Evangelism in a Skeptical World, Sam Chan, Zondervan, 2020 (excellent primer on sharing your faith).

Out of the Saltshaker and Into the World: Evangelism as a Way of Life, Rebecca Manley Pippert, IVP Signature Edition, 2021 (a timeless classic on effective faith-sharing).

Stay Salt: The World Has Changed, Our Message Must Not, Rebecca Manley Pippert, The Good Book Company, 2020 (highly informative and inspirational book on personal evangelism).

The Reluctant Witness: Discovering the Delight of Spiritual Conversations, Don Everts, IVP Books, 2019, (inspiring account of a real-world evangelistic opportunity and how God used it).

Master Plan of Evangelism, Robert Coleman, Second Edition, Revell, 2010, (a must-read classic on Jesus' plan for exponential evangelism).

Tell Someone: You Can Share the Good News, Greg Laurie, B&H Books, 2016 (basics of sharing our faith from a pastor and evangelist who reaches thousands).

Honest Evangelism: How to Talk about Jesus Even When It's Tough, Rico Tice, The Good Book Company, 2015 (encouragement from a proven veteran of evangelism).

Sharing Jesus (Without Freaking Out), Alvin L. Reid, B&H Academic, 2017 (helpful tips for natural outreach).

Organic Outreach for Ordinary People: Sharing Good News Naturally, Kevin G. Harney, Zondervan, 2018 (proven outreach principles from a pastor who really lives them).

BLESS: 5 Everyday Ways to Love Your Neighbor and Change the World, Dave Ferguson and Jon Ferguson, Salem Books, 2021 (a practical plan from two highly effective church leaders).

The Gospel Comes with a House Key: Practicing Radically

Ordinary Hospitality in Our Post-Christian World, Rosaria Butterfield, Crossway, 2018 (inspiring stories of the *Friendship-Building* and *Selfless-Serving* approaches that God used to reach people who were far from him).

Truth Plus Love: The Jesus Way to Influence, Matt Brown, Zondervan, 2019 (an encouraging book about two essential—but often missing—elements for sharing Christ with others).

The 9 Arts of Spiritual Conversations, Mary Schaller and John Crilly, Tyndale Momentum, 2016 (unpacks key elements of evangelistic relationships and discussions).

SHARE: A Field Guide to Sharing Your Faith, Greg Stier, Focus on the Family, 2006 (practical advice from a seasoned evangelism practitioner and trainer).

The Fuel & the Flame: Ignite Your Life & Your Campus for Jesus Christ, Steve Shadrach and Paul Worcester, CMM Press, 2021 (wisdom on reaching college students withe the gospel and training them to do the same.

Questioning Evangelism: Engaging People's Hearts the Way Jesus Did, Randy Newman, Kregel, 2019 (lessons from Jesus on how we can use questions to guide people to truth—and to him).

Tactics, 10th Anniversary Edition: A Game Plan for Discussing Your Christian Convictions, Gregory Koukl, Zondervan, 2019 (a proven field guide for defending your beliefs and pointing people back to the one who *is* the truth).

Evangelism Strategy and Trends

Becoming a Contagious Church: Increasing Your Church's Evangelistic Temperature, Mark Mittelberg, Zondervan, 2007 (a proven blueprint for helping your church or ministry prioritize evangelism and reach the people around you).

Organic Outreach for Churches: Infusing Evangelistic Passion in Your Local Congregation, Kevin G. Harney, Zondervan, Enlarged Edition, 2018 (expert advice on creating a culture of outreach in your congregation).

Seeker Small Groups, Garry Poole, Zondervan, 2003 (groundbreaking book on how we can reach people through spiritual discussion groups).

You Found Me: New Research on How Unchurched Nones, Millennials, and Irreligious Are Surprisingly Open to Christian Faith, Rick Richardson, IVP, 2019 (encouraging assessment of younger people's receptivity to the gospel).

Reviving Evangelism: Current Realities That Demand a New Vision for Sharing Faith, Barna Report, Produced in Partnership with Alpha USA, 2019 (sobering study of current patterns and attitudes related to evangelism, along with seasoned wisdom on how to move forward).

Your Spiritual Birthday: Rejoice and Celebrate, James B. Siebken, Equip Press, 2019 (inspiring insights on how we can utilize spiritual birthdays to promote both evangelism and discipleship).

Books on Evidence for the Christian Faith

The Questions Christians Hope No One Will Ask (With Answers), Mark Mittelberg, Tyndale, 2010 (answers and advice for addressing the ten questions that we're most afraid of).

Confident Faith: Building a Firm Foundation for Your Beliefs, Mark Mittelberg, Tyndale, 2013 (insights on ways people adopt their beliefs and how we can guide them onto more reliable pathways to truth; includes Mark's twenty reasons we can be confident Christianity is trustworthy).

The Case for Christ: A Journalist's Personal Investigation of the Evidence for Jesus, Lee Strobel, Zondervan, Updated and Expanded Edition, 2016 (the inspiring story of an atheist who researched the evidence for Christ and ended up as one of his followers, and who is now active in reaching others).

The Case for Christ Daily Moment of Truth, Lee Strobel and Mark Mittelberg, Zondervan, 2018 (180 readings that provide regular infusions of biblical truth and the evidence that backs it up).

Cold-Case Christianity: A Homicide Detective Investigates the Claims of the Gospel, J. Warner Wallace, David C. Cook, 2013 (powerful evidence for Christianity from a former detective).

On Guard: Defending Your Faith with Reason and Precision, William Lane Craig, David C. Cook, 2010 (evidence and answers from a leading Christian philosopher and professor).

I Don't Have Enough Faith to Be an Atheist, Norman Geisler and Frank Turek, Crossway, 2004 (a creative and powerful presentation on the top areas of evidence supporting the Christian faith).

Evidence that Demands a Verdict, Josh and Sean McDowell, Thomas Nelson, 2017 (the completely updated classic that presents compelling evidence for biblical belief).

Evidence for God: 50 Arguments for Faith from The Bible, History, Philosophy, And Science, William A. Dembski and Michael R. Licona, Baker Books, 2010 (presents an array of arguments and evidence from an impressive list of leading scholars).

Another Gospel?: A Lifelong Christian Seeks Truth in Response to Progressive Christianity, Alisa Childers, Tyndale, 2020 (insightful answers for those who encourage others to "reconstruct" and thus undermine their biblical beliefs).

Saving Truth: Finding Meaning and Clarity in a Post-Truth World, Abdu Murray, Zondervan, 2018 (a brilliant defense of objective truth in an era of radical relativism).

So the Next Generation Will Know: Preparing Young Christians for a Challenging World, Sean McDowell and J. Warner Wallace, David C. Cook, 2019 (essential information for reaching and equipping new generations).

Mama Bear Apologetics: Empowering Your Kids to Challenge Cultural Lies, Hillary Morgan Ferrer, gen. ed., Harvest House, 2019 (insights and advice from well-informed Christian moms who have learned to equip their children to prevail against challenges to their Christian faith).

Keeping Your Kids on God's Side: 40 Conversations to Help Them Build a Lasting Faith, Natasha Crain, Harvest House, 2016 (vital help for parents in teaching their kids the truth about Christianity).

Books on the Gospel

The King Jesus Gospel: The Original Good News Revisited, Scot McKnight, Zondervan, 2016 (a study of the gospel in its original context, and how we can better communicate it today).

Simply Good News: Why the Gospel Is News and What Makes It Good, N. T. Wright, HarperOne, 2015 (a fresh look at the biblical gospel and how we can effectively convey it to others).

What Is the Gospel?, Greg Gilbert, Crossway, 2010 (a review of key elements of the message of salvation).

Atonement and the Death of Christ: An Exegetical, Historical, and Philosophical Exploration, William Lane Craig, Baylor University Press, 2010 (a study of the core elements and meaning of Jesus's death).

The Cross of Christ, Jon Stott, Stott Centennial Edition, IVP, 2021 (this classic unpacks the biblical meaning and application of the crucifixion of Christ).

The Reason Why: Faith Makes Sense, Mark Mittelberg, Tyndale, 2011 (an introductory look at the gospel and the logic that supports it).

One-Verse Evangelism, Randy Raysbrook and Steve Walker, NavPress, 2013 (a creative and effective presentation of the gospel using Romans 6:23).

Evangelistic Books to Give to Friends

The Reason Why: Faith Makes Sense, Mark Mittelberg, Tyndale, 2011 (explains how the death of Jesus some two thousand years ago is relevant to our lives and futures today. Mark wrote this to be a small and affordable book that introduces people to our Christian faith).

The Case for Christ: A Journalist's Personal Investigation of the Evidence for Jesus, Lee Strobel, Zondervan, Updated and Expanded Edition, 2016 (this book has blessed and informed millions of believers, but it's also a fantastic tool for reaching friends who don't yet know Christ). Also, highly recommended: *The Case for Christ movie* from PureFlix, 2017, available on DVD or on-demand.

The Case for Hope: Looking Ahead with Confidence and Courage, Lee Strobel, Zondervan, 2022 (points to the truth of Christ as the reason for hope—now and into eternity).

The Case for Christianity Answer Book, Lee Strobel, Zondervan, 2014 (a great little tool for helping friends address and remove the intellectual roadblocks keeping them from faith).

The Case for Christmas: A Journalist Investigates the Identity of the Child in the Manger, Lee Strobel, Zondervan 2014 (an affordable outreach tool to give others around the Christmas holiday).

The Case for Easter: A Journalist Investigates Evidence for the Resurrection, Lee Strobel, Zondervan, 2009, (an effective and inexpensive outreach book to give others around Easter).

More Than a Carpenter, Josh and Sean McDowell, Tyndale Momentum, 2009 (this is a proven outreach tool that defends Jesus as the Son of God and the Savior of the world—and countless people have come to faith over the years after reading it).

Stories of Transformed Lives

The Case for Grace: A Journalist Explores the Evidence of Transformed Lives, Lee Strobel, Zondervan, 2015 (inspiring accounts of how God has reached and renewed the lives of many, often in dire circumstances).

Seeking Allah, Finding Jesus: A Devout Muslim Encounters Christianity, Nabeel Qureshi, Zondervan, 2014 (a loving and logical account of one man's journey from Islam to Christianity).

Unlikely Fighter: The Story of How a Fatherless Street Kid Overcame Violence, Chaos & Confusion to Become a Radical Christ Follower, Greg Stier, Tyndale, 2021 (the surprising spiritual story of the man we met in chapter 7, Greg Stier, who found Christ after his "Uncle Jack" came to faith).

Start Where You Are, Rashawn Copeland, Baker, 2020 (Rashawn started in a setting far from God, but today is a pastor who urges others to start where they are, but to let God take them where they need to go).

I Am Second: Real Stories. Changing Lives., Doug Bender and David Sterrett, Thomas Nelson, 2013 (testimonies from a variety of well-known people who chose to put Christ first in their lives).

Evangelism-Related Websites

ContagiousFaith.net (information and stories related to the *Contagious Faith* book and training course).

MarkMittelberg.com (the website for Mark Mittelberg, the author of this book and training course).

LeeStrobel.com (the website for the apologist and author, Lee Strobel).

StrobelCenter.com (the website for the Lee Strobel Center for Evangelism and Applied Apologetics at Colorado Christian University, where you can get online accredited or certificate training in these areas, and even discover some possible career opportunities).

DareToShare.com (this is Greg Stier's ministry, which trains high school students to share their faith. They also offer a helpful free evangelistic app, called "Life in 6 Words").

Groundwire.net (Groundwire is a ministry that reaches out to students with the gospel, providing them with resources and opportunities to chat with a coach about their spiritual questions and concerns).

AllAboutGod.com (All About God is the portal into a collection of websites designed to answer people's spiritual questions and point them to the truth of Christ and the gospel).

Thinke.org (Think Eternity is Matt Brown's ministry and website, and a great place for encouragement both for your faith and your outreach efforts).

CopelandMinistries.org (the online hub of Rashawn Copeland's extensive and multi-pronged outreach ministry).

Outreach.com (Outreach provides a wide variety of resources and communication tools to help you and your church or ministry reach out with the gospel).

ReasonableFaith.com (the online presence of Christian philosopher William Lane Craig, who defends the Christian faith against the toughest of challengers).

ColdCaseChristianity.com (the ministry of former cold-case detective-turned apologist J. Warner Wallace, who makes his case for the Christian faith with the goal of leading people to faith in Christ).

SeanMcDowell.org (the ministry of Sean McDowell, whose passion is to equip the church, and in particular young people, to make the case for the Christian faith).

AlisaChilders.com (the ministry of Alisa Childers, who defends the faith from the challenges of progressive Christianity).

CrossExamined.org (the ministry of Frank Turek, who defends and debates the truth of Christianity against a variety of challengers).

Cru.org (the online hub of Campus Crusade for Christ, now called Cru, which takes the gospel to universities and through a wide variety of ministries throughout the world).

InterVarsity.org (InterVarsity is a university-based ministry that reaches and teaches the faith to students).

Navigators.org (The Navigators are all about making and training disciples at colleges and universities).

RatioCristi.org (a network of ministry chapters that teach and defend Christian truth on college campuses).

STR.org (the online hub of Greg Koukl and his Stand to Reason ministry team).

Reasons.org (the online hub of Hugh Ross and his Reasons to Believe ministry team).

Summit.org (Summit Ministries has been offering world class worldview training for high school and college-aged students for more than 60 years, as well as publishing excellent training books and videos).

ColsonCenter.org (the Colson Center, the ministry launched by the late Charles Colson, which trains and informs Christians about issues relevant to living out our faith in secular culture).

WheatonBillyGraham.com (the Billy Graham Center at Wheaton College is a hub of evangelism training and activities).

BillyGraham.org (the Billy Graham Evangelistic Association was established years ago by Billy Graham, and provides a variety of outreach resources, training, and information).

Palau.org (founded by Luis Palau and his sons, provides a variety of evangelism resources and connections).

Harvest.org (the ministry of Greg Laurie, Harvest leads and promotes evangelism throughout North America).

Alpha.org (the online hub of the international Alpha ministry, which hosts the Alpha Course that is reaching countless people around the globe).

ChristianityExplored.org (the online hub of the international Christianity Explored ministry, which hosts Christianity Explored small groups that are reaching people around the world).

OneLifeAdvisors.com (Garry Poole's One Life Advisors ministry, which provides seasoned evangelistic coaching and ideas for churches).

QPlace.com (the online hub of the Q Place ministry, which trains and supports people in leading Q Place evangelistic small groups from their homes, offices, and churches).

WhosYourOne.com (this site encourages believers all over North America to register the name of one friend or acquaintance who they'll commit to praying for in order to lead that person to Christ).

NOTES

Our Contagious Calling

1. *Merriam-Webster.com Dictionary*, Merriam-Webster, https://www
.merriam-webster.com/dictionary/contagious. Accessed June 1, 2020.

Chapter 1: Reached by God to Reach Others

1. Steve Macchia, *Becoming a Healthy Church* (Grand Rapids, MI: Baker, 1999), 139.

2. Ed Stetzer, "7 Reasons Evangelism Has Declined in the Church," *Outreach Magazine*, February 2, 2020. It can be read at: https:// outreachmagazine.com/features/evangelism/51409-7-reasons
-evangelism-has-declined-in-the-church.html.

3. "Evangelicals deeply confused about core Christian beliefs," by *Religious News LLC*, October 16, 2018. Viewable at: https:// religionnews.com/2018/10/16/evangelicals-deeply-confuse
-about-core-christian-beliefs/.

4. Cliffe Knechtle, *Give Me an Answer* (Downers Grove, IL: InterVarsity Press, 1986), 164.

Chapter 2: Finding an Approach That Fits You

1. *LifeWay Research*, April 23, 2019, "Evangelism More Prayed for Than Practiced by Churchgoers," online at: https:// lifewayresearch.com/2019/04/23/evangelism-more-prayed
-for-than-practiced-by-churchgoers/.

2. I am deeply grateful to Bill Hybels for his groundbreaking

sermon that night at Willow Creek, and for all the ways God
used his insights on styles of evangelism—both for me and for
the many others we were able to encourage later through our
book, *Becoming a Contagious Christian* (Grand Rapids, MI:
Zondervan, 1994).

3. See: www.StrobelCenter.com.

Chapter 3: Style #1: Friendship-Building

1. For a great discussion on the benefits of remembering and
commemorating people's spiritual birthdays, see James
B. Siebken, *Your Spiritual Birthday: Rejoice and Celebrate*
(Colorado Springs: Equip Press, 2019).

2. You can discover the details of Lee Strobel's journey to faith in
his bestselling book, *The Case for Christ*, or by watching the
award-winning movie with the same title.

3. From the video, "A Gift of a Bible," viewable on YouTube at:
https://www.youtube.com/watch?v=6md638smQd8.

Chapter 4: Style #2: Selfless-Serving

1. *Merriam-Webster.com Dictionary*, Merriam-Webster, https://www
.merriam-webster.com/dictionary/empathy. Accessed June 1, 2020.

2. Lee Strobel and Mark Mittelberg, *The Case for Christ Daily
Moment of Truth* (Grand Rapids, MI: Zondervan, 2016),
132–133.

3. Kevin Harney, *No Is a Beautiful Word: Hope and Help for the
Overcommitted and (Occasionally) Exhausted* (Grand Rapids, MI:
Zondervan, 2019), 22.

4. "Pat Boone believes that he will meet Hollywood star, Rock
Hudson, again in heaven," by Dan Wooding, *Assist News Service*,
March 19, 2018 (viewable at: https://www.assistnews.net/pat
-boone-believes-that-he-will-meet-hollywood-star-rock-hudson
-again-in-heaven/). Pat Boone also discusses this in his book, *Pat
Boone's America—50 Years* (Nashville: B&H Publishing Group,
2006), 142.

Chapter 5: Style #3: Story-Sharing

1. Lee Strobel, speaking at Saddleback Church in Lake Forest, California, May 14, 2016, in a message called, "Learn How Jesus Brings Clarity to Your Questions," viewable at https://youtu.be/EUlBjUr5jKk.
2. Lee Strobel, *The Case for Christ*, updated and expanded edition (Grand Rapids, MI: Zondervan, 1998, 2016), 14.
3. Ibid., 287.
4. Karen Lee-Thorp, *How to Ask Great Questions* (Colorado Springs: NavPress, 1998), 50–5, as quoted by Garry Poole, *Seeker Small Groups* (Grand Rapids, MI: Zondervan, 2003), 122, 312.
5. Garry Poole, *Seeker Small Groups* (Grand Rapids, MI: Zondervan, 2003), 122–123.
6. This is from Garry Poole's handouts at seminars he teaches, as communicated to Mark Mittelberg in an email.
7. Lee Strobel and Mark Mittelberg, *Making Your Case for Christ* (Grand Rapids, MI: Zondervan, 2018), Session 2, 29, 34–35.
8. Mark Mittelberg, the *Contagious Faith Training Course* six-week video curriculum, which includes printed study guides for each group member and streaming or DVD video training from Mittelberg and guests (Grand Rapids, MI: HarperChristian Resources, 2021).
9. *Guinness World Records*, accessed December 14, 2020, www.guinnessworldrecords.com/records-11000/most-broken-bones-in-a-lifetime.
10. Story of Evel Knievel adapted from Lee Strobel, *The Case for Hope* (Grand Rapids, MI: Zondervan, 2015), 159–163.

Chapter 6: Style #4: Reason-Giving

1. Again, this is the central purpose of the Lee Strobel Center for Evangelism and Applied Apologetics at Colorado Christian University. At both the undergraduate and graduate levels, as well as the certificate level (for those who just want the practical training), we're offering online courses in the areas of Practical

Apologetics, Global Apologetics, Cultural Engagement, and Innovative Evangelism. For more information see StrobelCenter .com.

2. Mark Mittelberg, *The Questions Christians Hope No One Will Ask (With Answers)* (Carol Stream, IL: Tyndale, 2010).

3. Here are two excellent guides to help you ask great questions in order to deepen your spiritual interactions: *Questioning Evangelism: Engaging People's Hearts the Way Jesus Did*, by Randy Newman (2nd edition, Kregel, 2017), and *Tactics: A Game Plan for Discussing Your Christian Convictions*, by Greg Koukl (10th anniversary edition, Grand Rapids, MI: Zondervan, 2019).

Chapter 7: Style #5: Truth-Telling

1. You can read about Stier's fascinating journey in his autobiography, Greg Stier, *Unlikely Fighter: The Story of How a Fatherless Street Kid Overcame Violence, Chaos & Confusion to Become a Radical Christ Follower* (Carol Stream, IL: Tyndale, 2021).

2. For more information about Greg Stier's ministry, Dare 2 Share, and to get details on their training events and published resources, go to www.dare2share.org.

An Epidemic of Spiritual Influence

1. Malcolm Gladwell, *The Tipping Point: How Little Things Can Make a Big Difference* (New York: Little, Brown and Company, Time Warner Group, 2002), 9.

Chapter 8: Understanding and Applying the Gospel

1. Scot McKnight, *The King Jesus Gospel: The Original Good News Revisited, Revised Edition* (Grand Rapids, MI: Zondervan, 2011, 2016). My thanks to Dr. McKnight for his biblical insights, and to John Raymond at Zondervan for alerting me to the importance of the message in his book. I should add that I also found helpful information in N. T. Wright, *Simply Good News:*

Why the Gospel Is News, and What Makes It Good (New York: HarperCollins, 2015) as well as Matthew W. Bates, *Gospel Allegiance* (Grand Rapids, MI: Baker, 2019).

2. McKnight, *King Jesus Gospel*, 55.
3. James D. G. Dunn, *Jesus Remembered* (Grand Rapids, MI: Eerdmans, 2003) 854–55, emphasis mine.
4. Ibid., 53.
5. Note: This outline follows the general pattern of McKnight and others (see, for example, *King Jesus Gospel*, 53), leaning heavily on Paul's explanation of the gospel in 1 Corinthians 15.
6. Matthew W. Bates, *Gospel Allegiance* (Grand Rapids, MI: Baker, 2019) heightened my awareness of this term and concept.
7. Note: Lee Strobel and I unpack this illustration in our video discussion guide, *Making Your Case for Christ*, Session 5, "Explaining the Central Message of Christ," 89ff. Also, this illustration was helpful to Strobel when he actually came to faith years ago, as portrayed in the movie "The Case for Christ," (Scottsdale, AZ: PureFlix, 2017).
8. Strobel and Mittelberg, *Making Your Case for Christ*, 102–103.
9. Nabeel Qureshi, *No God But One: A Former Muslim Investigates the Evidence for Islam & Christianity* (Grand Rapids, MI: Zondervan, 2016), 152–153.

Chapter 9: When Your Style Doesn't Fit the Situation

1. Rebecca Manley Pippert, *Stay Salt* (Charlotte, NC: The Good Book Company, 2020), 62–64.

Chapter 10: Experiencing the Unexpected Adventure

1. *Merriam-Webster.com Dictionary*, Merriam-Webster, https://www .merriam-webster.com/dictionary/adventure. Accessed June 1, 2020.
2. Eugene H. Peterson, *Traveling Light: Modern Meditations on St. Luke's Letters of Freedom* (Downers Grove, IL: InterVarsity, 1988), 45.
3. See: https://www.palau.org/about.

4. Lee Strobel and Mark Mittelberg, *The Unexpected Adventure: Taking Everyday Risks to Talk to People about Jesus* (Grand Rapids, MI: Zondervan, 2007), 14.

5. Mark Mittelberg, *Contagious Faith Training Course* six-week video curriculum (Grand Rapids, MI: HarperChristian Resources, 2021).

Chapter 11: Leaving a Lasting Legacy

1. "World Christian Growth Statistics!" Prayer Foundation, http://www.prayerfoundation.org/world_christian_growth_statistics.htm, as cited in Michael L. Brown and Craig Keener, *Not Afraid of the Antichrist* (Grand Rapids, MI: Baker Publishing Group, 2019), 197.

2. Ibid., 198 (citing "State of the World: Growth of the Church," The Traveling Team, http://www.thetravelingteam.org/articles/growth-of-the-church).

3. Ibid., 198.

MEET MARK MITTELBERG

Mark Mittelberg is a bestselling author, international speaker, and executive director of the Lee Strobel Center for Evangelism and Applied Apologetics at Colorado Christian University.

He was the primary author of the celebrated *Becoming a Contagious Christian* training course, which was translated into 20 languages and used by nearly two million people around the world. He has now developed the all-new *Contagious Faith* book and video training course, as well as *Becoming a Contagious Church*, which presents an innovative blueprint for church-based evangelism.

Mark's books also include *The Unexpected Adventure* and *The Case for Christ Daily Moment of Truth* devotional (both with Lee Strobel); *The Questions Christians Hope No One Will Ask (With Answers)*, winner of the Retailers Choice Award; and *Confident Faith*, winner of *Outreach Magazine's* Apologetics Book of the Year.

Mark was the original evangelism director at Willow Creek Community Church in Chicago. He then served as executive vice president of the Willow Creek Association, leading in the area of outreach for more than 10,000 member churches. He was also an editorial consultant and periodic guest for Lee Strobel's television show, *Faith Under Fire*. He and Strobel have been ministry partners for more than thirty years.

After completing an undergraduate degree in business, Mark earned an MA in Philosophy of Religion from Trinity International University in Deerfield, Illinois. He also received an honorary Doctor of Divinity degree from Southern Evangelical Seminary. Mark and Heidi live near Denver, Colorado, and are the parents of two grown children, Emma Jean and Matthew, both of whom serve in ministry roles.

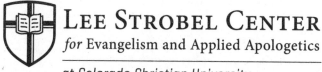

New Video Study for Your Church or Small Group

If you've enjoyed this book, now you can go deeper with the companion video Bible study!

In this six-session study, Mark Mittelberg helps you apply the principles in *Contagious Faith* to your life. The study guide includes streaming video access, video teaching notes, group discussion questions, personal reflection questions, and a leader's guide.

Study Guide plus
Streaming Video
9780310121909

DVD
9780310121923

Available now at your favorite bookstore,
or streaming video on StudyGateway.com.